# Miracle in the Mine

# Miracle *in the* Mine

ONE MAN'S STORY OF
STRENGTH & SURVIVAL
IN THE CHILEAN MINES

JOSÉ HENRÍQUEZ

ZONDERVAN®

ZONDERVAN.com/
AUTHORTRACKER
*follow your favorite authors*

We want to hear from you. Please send your comments about this book to us in care of zreview@zondervan.com. Thank you.

ZONDERVAN

*Miracle in the Mine*
Copyright © 2011 by José Henríquez

This title is also available as a Zondervan ebook.
Visit www.zondervan.com/ebooks.

This title is also available in a Zondervan audio edition.
Visit www.zondervan.fm.

Requests for information should be addressed to:
Zondervan, Grand Rapids, Michigan 49530

ISBN 978-0-310-33640-2

International Trade Paper Edition

All Scripture quotations, unless otherwise indicated, are taken from The Holy Bible, *New International Version®, NIV®*. Copyright © 1973, 1978, 1984, 2011 by Biblica, Inc.™ Used by permission. All rights reserved worldwide.

Any Internet addresses (websites, blogs, etc.) and telephone numbers in this book are offered as a resource. They are not intended in any way to be or imply an endorsement by Zondervan, nor does Zondervan vouch for the content of these sites and numbers for the life of this book.

*Cover design: Michelle Lenger*
*Front cover photography: © Claudio Reyes / epa / Corbis*
*Back cover photography: © Marcelo Hernandez / dpa / Corbis*
*Photo of Mr. Henríquez: Copyright © 2011 John Carins Photography*
*Interior design: Beth Shagene*
*Insert photography: Unless otherwise indicated, provided*
*by the Henríquez family*

*Printed in the United States of America*

11 12 13 14 15 16 /DCI/ 20 19 18 17 16 15 14 13 12 11 10 9 8 7 6 5 4 3 2 1

*To the glory and honor*
*of our Lord Jesus Christ*

# Contents

# CHAPTER 1

## The Miracles Unfold

Beginning at midnight on Wednesday, October 13, 2010, the entire world witnessed a rescue unlike anything ever seen before. The unprecedented operation to rescue thirty-three miners who had been trapped for nearly seventy days was expected to take about forty-eight hours. More than three hundred million television viewers attentively watched every move made by the rescue team. Those of us trapped in the depths of the San José mine also watched every detail eagerly. Our lives depended on this rescue, and nothing was certain.

Nothing had been certain since the moment the mine collapsed on Thursday, August 5, 2010. We felt the earth shake when that terrible event confined thirty-three of us inside a chasm 2,300 feet underground. Rescue workers began searching for survivors the following day, but on August 7, only a day and a half after the first collapse, a second collapse occurred while rescuers were trying to enter through the mine's ventilation shaft.

At the top of the mine, the situation was desperate. A wall of debris almost a half mile thick blocked the entrance. To continue the rescue effort, it became necessary to bring heavy machinery to the mine, which was located about eighteen and a half miles northeast of the city of Copiapó in Chile.

Below the surface, the situation was even more desperate. We were not found alive until Sunday, August 22, seventeen days after the initial collapse. The confirmation of our survival was only the beginning of an epic struggle for our families, the rescue workers, our nation, and all of those hoping for our rescue. We were alive — but entombed! We needed a solid faith to harbor at least a thread of hope that any positive outcome could result from this nightmarish event and that at least some of us would be able to once again feel the rays of the sun warming our faces.

From the time we were found, we waited for another seven and a half weeks to be rescued! As we waited, the minutes seemed like hours, the hours like days, and the days changed us forever. After what seemed like endless days of arduous labor — labor that bordered on the sacrificial in order to accomplish the drilling and casing of a duct linking us to the surface — it was announced that the rescue would begin. Finally, about ten minutes after the scheduled starting time, the first survivor was raised to the surface. The rest of us followed soon after, at the pace of about one man every hour.

*Our rescue was just one of many miracles that took place in that mine.*

Many have said that the successful rescue of all thirty-three Chilean miners from the San José mine was a miracle. And it was. But our rescue was just one of many miracles that took place in that mine and in the lives of those who lived through that ordeal. For me, that miracle began in February 1957.

## My Childhood and Youth

My life began in the village of San Clemente, in the province of Talca, near the mountains, part of Chile's Seventh Region of Maule. I come from a family of eleven siblings, although only seven of us remain. Because we were a Christian family, my parents named each of us after Bible characters. One is named Elijah, another Esther, and so on. I am José, named after Joseph.

My relationship with my mother was always very good. My mother always wanted the best for her children. She was good to us but also strict. When we were young, she imposed strict discipline and punished us when necessary. I truly believe that one of the most wonderful things for a son is to have his mother. As sons, we do not always understand this when we are adolescents, but we do know this when we are children and later when we are adults.

My relationship with my father was different. He often treated me harshly, and perhaps that is why at times I also am harsh. However, my father took us to see interesting places, such as the central hydroelectric plant called El Toro and the city of Los Ángeles, which was very exciting for me. During my teenage years, when we lived in Los Ángeles in the region of Biobío, I saw very little of him. Because of his work, he came home only once a month. Adolescence is one of the most complicated stages of life, and a boy needs his father around to talk to him. So in terms of having a father during that time of life, I felt somewhat alone.

I really would have liked to have spent more time near my father. But on the positive side, his prolonged absences contributed to a strong relationship with my grandfather, who was a pastor.

My close relationship with my grandfather was part of God's purpose because it allowed me to learn about the Lord. Many times I saw my grandfather go through difficult situations because of the gospel. He experienced many times of need. Nevertheless, he continued to preach the gospel with great love.

I sometimes went with my grandfather to prayer vigils and church services in the mountainous areas. I also went with him to remote villages where he went to proclaim the gospel. We often arrived home late at night and sometimes turned around just a few hours later to go out to other locations. On some occasions we traveled together by bicycle, and at times we walked all night long to get to a village.

My grandfather was a very tolerant and loving pastor. He had a beautiful way of relating to people. He knew how to sympathize with people and how to influence them. He knew how to present Christ. He preached with much virtue and was dearly loved in the hills and the countryside where he carried out his ministry. Because of these qualities I became very close to him. For a long time I have acknowledged him as the spiritual leader of my life. His example often came to mind during my days in the dark passageways of the San José mine.

# The Music of My Life

My grandfather also shared with me a love for music and the gift of playing the accordion. Much of what I learned came by watching him play his instrument and hearing him sing. While attending school in Los Ángeles, I also learned to play guitar, drums, and other musical instruments. When we lived in Talca, I began to perform with folk music ensembles. Soon music became the most important thing in my life.

I loved the cueca, which is the national dance of Chile, and I was very skilled on the harp, guitar, and accordion. By age eighteen, I helped to organize a folk music ensemble. Our ensemble earned two important awards in the category of cueca at the Copihue de Oro, an annual musical contest.

Our music took us to many places, including to Argentina. For many years we performed in San Bernardo, where folk ensembles gather to perform. An arts festival held there highlights the best of folk music. Forgotten works are recovered and restaged. Exhibitions highlight paintings and art works from various regions of the country. Research is done and contributions are made to musical culture.

It was an exciting time for us to share the beautiful Chilean music that we loved, but man always has a way of wasting things. And that is what happened to me. Folk music did not bring meaning to my life, nor did it give me satisfaction. I dedicated seventeen years of my life to music, but I was not fulfilled. My life seemed empty.

Our music also took me down roads that led me away from God. My brother, who performed folk music with me, and I often argued about the themes of the songs we performed. Even though at that time in our lives we were looking for satisfaction outside the church, the music of our grandfather was still part of the melody in our hearts and minds. Whenever we heard Christian music, we immediately found agreement. Instantly, any enmity between us would cease. This helped me to understand the meaning of the Scripture that tells us that our Lord inhabits the praises of his people (Psalm 22:3). I found that if you take a guitar or an accordion and play for Christ, you will encounter him in the midst of your praises. I have always found this to be true, even in the middle of a dark mine.

Although I distanced myself from the church and devoted myself to music, I always maintained a very close relationship with my grandfather. He tolerated me for many years, even when he saw my mistakes. He never judged me. He supported me and taught me many things. He never stopped loving me and always had a very good attitude toward me. His presence filled my life with grace and surrounded me with love. Just as the Lord Jesus came to rescue and save that which was lost, my grandfather rescued me with love.

In time, love won me over. Although many of us want to say, "I believe in God, but I do not want to obey him," we must accept his Word, his precepts, his commandments, his statutes in order to believe in him. We cannot say that we believe in God if we will not let him be the Lord of our lives. Without faith it is impossible to please God. The Bible declares, "Faith comes from hearing the message, and the message is heard through the word about Christ" (Romans 10:17).

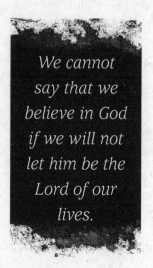

*We cannot say that we believe in God if we will not let him be the Lord of our lives.*

As we grow in our knowledge of the Word of God, we come to a better understanding of these things. Little by little, God gives us more understanding and wisdom as he prepares us for greater challenges. During the years in which I was playing music, I never thought I would preach on the streets. I never thought I would preach in a mine.

God did this for me because this is how he rescues us for new opportunities.

My story with God began long before the collapse of the San José mine. As we miners waited 2,300 feet below the earth's surface, we could hear the pounding heartbeats of our companions in that small, enclosed space. We knew that a miracle was happening. The challenges of our long ordeal were finally coming to an end, but we were anxious about the journey ahead. None of us knew what the future would hold. When my turn came to step out of the rescue capsule, I was utterly amazed to see all of the equipment that God had assembled to save our lives. I realized that God had counted no cost too great to rescue us (the rescue operation was estimated to cost about twenty million dollars). I sensed that the miraculous rescue from our ordeal was not the end, but it marked the beginning of new opportunities for each of us.

# CHAPTER 2

## Training for
## the San José Mine

Despite my opportunities to play folk music at rodeos and festivals, music could not fill my heart. But I can say that something wonderful came out of the time I devoted to performing folk music, and that is the fact that at a festival I met and fell in love with a folk dancer by the name of Hettiz Berrios Vásquez, the woman who is my wife.

After we had been in a dating relationship for some time, I told my father that I wanted to get married. From the beginning my family accepted Hettiz, and she knew that we were Christians. I wanted to get married and be the proper head of my family. I could not live on music alone, so it became necessary to find a steady job with a salary in order to realize my dream of having a family.

Because I had studied mechanics, I went to

large workshops to look for work on ship mechanics. I presented my résumé and curriculum vitae at every place I thought I could possibly find work. I asked everyone to give me an opportunity to introduce myself and to put forward my recommendations as a good worker. I believed that these, together with my testimony, would speak well for me. Even though I was not close to the Lord at the time, the teachings of my family were always present in my life. The Word states, "Let someone else praise you, and not your own mouth; an outsider, and not your own lips" (Proverbs 27:2). With this in mind, I offered my résumé, hoping that with the passage of time my experience and good behavior would confirm my potential.

*The hope of seeing Hettiz again often warmed my heart during days of hardship and suffering inside the mines.*

I did not find the work I desired. Without contacts and friends who could help me from inside the ship mechanics business, the doors were closed to me. Finally, I took a job as a day laborer. Because I was very much in love and very much wanted to get married, I accepted a job in the mine called El Teniente

(The Lieutenant). That is how my life as a miner —
like that of my father, my uncles, and my brothers
— began.

## My Introduction to Old-Style Mining

My hard work in the mines began in 1974, but I did
not mind it because my desire and purpose was to
start a family. I knew that God blesses marriage,
and after so many years I can say that we have been
very happy. Hettiz has been the mainstay of my
life. She matches perfectly the biblical description
of the virtuous woman: "A wife of noble character
who can find? She is worth far more than rubies"
(Proverbs 31:10). I give thanks to God for the wife
that I have, and I feel very proud of her. The hope
of seeing her again often warmed my heart during
days of hardship and suffering inside the mines.

And there were plenty of days of hardship. At El
Teniente in Rancagua, in the province of Cachapoal,
I experienced what it means to work in old-style
mining. There, miners did everything manually,
with the pickax. For the twelve of us who started
the job together, our test of fire was a shovel. Each
team of four men was given a mine cart with a
capacity of eight tons. It had to be filled and ready

to go by noon each day. After our time of testing, only four out of the twelve remained.

I did not know very much about how to use the tools of mining, but my father had taught me a little. And because of the close relationship that I maintained with my grandfather, I have always been drawn to men who are much older and more experienced in their jobs. In this way I learned how to do mining from the masters. These experienced men taught me how to work with the machines and gave advice such as the proper grip to use for operating a certain machine. Their wisdom helped me to come out ahead. So I always encourage young people to approach their elders — those who know more — and to gain wisdom from them.

During my apprenticeship at El Teniente, I worked as a woodworker, deliveryman, sifter, and in a few other positions in the mine as well. At that time, we built all our own mine carts, and the woodworker was the one who repaired the doors. Now mine carts use hydraulic doors and other marvels of modern technology. The sifter position no longer exists. Miners use a hammer on the sifter that they can operate remotely via computer from an office at another location. But during my early days of mining, things were not done that way. The carts full of ore had to be emptied by hand, using wheelbarrows.

Later, I went to work for a contracting business. I moved to Los Ángeles, to Pichipolcura, and also to Lota and other cities where the business sent me to work on certain projects.

In the town of Lota, I worked in a carbon mine, where I had a very beautiful experience. Lota is considered a Christian town that has many churches. Many people there know Jesus and the things of God. The men there are very good men.

I believe Lota is the only place I have worked where the workers praised God before they entered the mine. We boarded a train at the access tunnel that took us to a point five and a half miles below sea level. That was the distance we had to travel just to get to where we worked! Because we were all Christians, we would sing to the Lord on the way. Before beginning our labors, we held a service to honor the Lord. Each day we sang songs of praise, read from Scripture, and prayed before we went to our work areas to begin our tasks.

We were very happy in Lota, but after a while, a representative from the company notified me that I was to move to Santiago to work in the gold mine El Indio in the area of La Serena. After leaving Lota, I began to notice how very merciful God had been to me. Mining work comes with a high risk of accidents, and I was exposed to accidents repeatedly.

*As children of God, we share in the bounties of the Father.*

But long before finding myself in the depths of the San José mine, I began to understand that even though we are imperfect, God loves us so much that he gives us his protection. As children of God, we share in the bounties of the Father — those bounties he owns and puts at our disposal. He often warns us about things before they happen. He shows his people his love when he sends his angels to protect us.

## Indebted to God at El Alfalfal

In 1986, I was part of a team that was building a hydroelectric plant at El Alfalfal, in the Metropolitan Region of Chile. One morning the strange image of a large cup full of concrete about to overflow came into my mind. At that time I remembered that the Word tells us, "The first angel went and poured out his bowl on the land" (Revelation 16:2). So I asked the Lord, "What does this mean?"

Then I remembered a plowman who had passed by the mine and warned that something was going to happen and that we were in danger at the mine.

No one paid attention to his warning, but an accident occurred the first night we slept in the mining camp. The following night another accident occurred — an avalanche of rocks falling rapidly down the mountainside, which brought flooding in the valley.

We were sound asleep when we suddenly felt a loud roar and then a shaking. It seemed worse than an earthquake. The whole camp was being tossed from side to side. My brother, who is also a Christian, was with me. He woke me up and said, "Come, look how the river is rising!"

The river was too swollen, and the campground was almost on top of the flowing current! The flood was coming from the far side. It had already covered some buildings, including a casino and the offices. I said to my brother and the people who were with us, "There is no time to gather anything. We must leave right now!"

As we ran the 200 yards toward the safety of a hill, the avalanche grew larger and larger. Several business buildings had been demolished and dragged into the floodwaters, as well as trucks, buses, and all kinds of machinery. The newspapers later printed a photograph of a huge stone about forty-two and a half feet in diameter that had been dislodged by the avalanche and was being pushed by the floodwaters!

As we ran, we paused to knock on the doors of some friends who were sleeping to try to awaken them so that they could get out, but we could do little more than shout and run. I will always remember Dinamarca, a friend from Antuco, who left his room and was running along with me. He fell. I helped him get up, and then he turned back.

"Where are you going?" I shouted.

He was still half asleep and did not understand the danger. He wanted to return to his room! I pleaded with him not to go back, but he ignored me, and I never saw him again.

We ran and ran. The hot stones burned the soles of our feet. We climbed around the side of the mountain, about 270 yards, and watched the flood pass. It was terrible. We stayed there all night, only partially clothed, petrified by fear and watching desperately as we saw the way our friends were dying. Many of the men who climbed into the hills later had to be brought down by helicopter because they could not descend from the mountain on their own.

The incident was very serious. More than fifty people died, although no one knows the exact number because many people were buried under the avalanche. Many of my friends lost their lives there. That is why I say I am very indebted to God. This would not be the only time that God saved me to continue writing his story with me.

## Trained in the Valley of the Shadow of Death

Anyone can be affected by tragedy in an instant, and we cannot explain why such things happen. Many people blame God for such tragedies, but in reality, man bears much of the guilt. Things like this sometimes happen because of man's irresponsibility in searching for economic opportunities without valuing life. Over and over again, I have seen the dire consequences that occur when human beings think only of protecting material things. After the flood at El Alfalfal, for example, everyone fought to rescue the mining company equipment without realizing that the victims' bodies were still inside and that the widows would be asking about their dead husbands.

During my life, I have worked at several mines —at the copper mine in Rancagua, a carbon mine in Lota, and a gold mine in La Escondida—and have seen death prowling nearby. The same year of the El Alfalfal flood, in the city of Santiago in the

Cajón del Maipo mining area, we witnessed an accident that killed half of the team of men working the night shift. Half of the team! That morning the foreman in charge was my father, whom God graciously guarded. At the El Teniente mine, located about fifty miles south of Santiago, God protected me from three explosions in the rocks and from another flood.

*Seeing the hand of God working in my life through all of these events has become more marvelous as time goes by.*

I also spent several years working in Chuquicamata as a driller, so I can confirm that the mining accidents I experienced prior to the one at the San José mine represent real-life training. I believe that these events in my life represent something similar to what it meant for David to slay lions and bears before he faced his fight with Goliath. Seeing the hand of God working in my life through all of these events has become more marvelous as time goes by. Even though I go through the valley of the shadow of death, I continue to have faith that God is at work in my life to accomplish his purpose.

# CHAPTER 3

## Under the Covering of God

The arrival of our daughters brought an unexpected surprise. It was quite a shock when we learned that we were going to have twins. A double portion of happiness was ours! But throughout the childhood of our daughters, my work as a miner took me away from home for days at a time.

The contracting jobs that I worked operated on a system of turns: eleven for three, eleven for six, ten for five, and twenty for ten. Turns consisted of twenty days of work followed by ten days of rest, or eleven days of work and six days of rest. Such prolonged work schedules are no longer allowed. Now miners work four for four — four days of work and four days of rest. The old system, working eleven days and resting six, was convenient for those of us who lived far away and had to travel long distances to reach the mine. Fewer return trips home allowed us to enjoy more time and rest at home.

My work schedule required my wife to assume most of the responsibility for raising our daughters. They are wonderful daughters who have always behaved very well. Although they missed having me at home, they did not complain when they learned that I had to leave again. We made the most of every opportunity when I was at home with them.

My life was never very difficult because my mother was always very good to me, and I was fortunate with my own family. My work was hard, but it was good work. Nevertheless, I was not happy. I did not feel fulfilled in my daily life. Family and work were not enough. Something was missing.

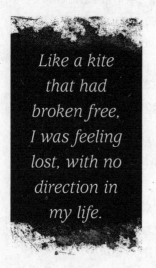

*Like a kite that had broken free, I was feeling lost, with no direction in my life.*

Soccer games and card games were never my comforts. Although I enjoyed playing music, which was a gift the Lord gave me to use for him, it did not satisfy me. Like many young people, I did not have a clear vision or a good direction, so I did not know what to do with the talents I had received or how to manage my life. But now I know that we can be confident that the Lord is in charge of these things. God allows us to fly free like a kite, lofted into the air until the rope breaks. And then he is there in his mercy to give us a new opportunity to fly under his control. Like a kite that had broken free, I was feeling lost, with no direction in my life. But something was about to happen.

## Stepping in a New Direction

Once again, God used my grandfather as the influence I desperately needed. My grandfather was a godly and wise man who was tolerant of my youthful vices. I was not a drinker, but I liked cigars and had a propensity for saying bad words. On one occasion he even gave me money to buy cigarettes because he knew that when a vice is operating in a man, he is dominated by it. My grandfather let me fly, just like a kite, so that I would see that the world could not satisfy.

One day, I went to the church my parents attended because the pastor, Osvaldo Real, had invited my grandfather to be there. I only went along to accompany my mother and to make sure that nothing happened to my grandfather on the way. I sat on a bench near the back of the church, as I usually did the few times I went. But on that particular Sunday, as we were leaving the building, my grandfather happily came over and hugged me and said, "And you, boy? With this body and such a coward! When are you going to accept the Lord Jesus Christ?"

I looked directly at him and thought, "What could this old man be thinking?" Of course I did not express this thought out loud, but it was what my heart was feeling. His words made me restless. I realized that I could no longer continue to live separated from God. Less than a week later, I asked my mother, "Well, what do I have to do to accept Jesus Christ? What do I have to do to serve God?"

> *When God begins to speak to our hearts, a work of transformation begins in every area of our lives.*

She said, "Take your accordion and go present yourself to the pastor. That is all you have to do."

I took her advice. That same day, I went to the pastor and began to experience a change in my life. A fire began to burn inside me. Even now I do not have the words to explain the great love that I received that day, a love that marked me forever.

Some people think they have to change first and then seek God, but the Lord tells us that we must seek him first and then he will help us to change. He tells us, "Come to me just as you are." He received me just as I was, with a mouth that spewed bad words, with my fingers yellowed and my breath smelling of cigars, and, most of all, with a heart that was unsatisfied.

God will not rule us by force. However, when I finally came to the point where I dared to say, "Here I am, Lord. I want to know you. I want to give you my life," God began to take charge of my existence. I was no longer a kite adrift on the breeze. God had taken hold of the string.

## My Transformation Begins

The jargon used by miners is very harsh and unpleasant. But when God begins to speak to our hearts, a work of transformation begins in every area of our lives. When I finally began to seek God's help and direction, I immediately began to see results. I learned that the Lord can change even our way of speaking, not just by the words themselves but by transforming what is in our hearts and what our words provoke in other people.

The week after I accepted the Lord in my life, I felt a great sense of shame about something I had done that served as a harsh lesson for me. I was operating a large drilling machine and was working with an assistant who was not the person I normally worked with. While we were in the middle of a task, I noticed that he was making a mistake. I made a very insulting comment about him — and I thank God that my coworker did not hear it! But with my renewed ears, *I* heard it, and what days earlier might have seemed normal to me now filled me with shame. I felt bad on the one hand, yet at the same time I immediately felt happy because I realized that God was giving me a new conscience to see with great clarity what is good.

From that day forward, the Lord changed my way of speaking. I acknowledged my sin, and he transformed me. Before that time, I could not speak without inserting about twenty or thirty vulgar expressions into everything I said. Now that the Lord was truly Lord of my life, I could no longer use this kind of vocabulary that presents a bad testimony to all around me. God was freeing me from that behavior because I had found "his wonderful light" (1 Peter 2:9).

I discovered that God deals with each one of us in a personal way. He is loving and kind. Little by little, through his Word and through love and carefulness, he will eliminate everything that is unpleasant in us. We never stop learning and being molded by him if we pay attention to the teachings in his Word. This is why it is so important to attend church—so we can come to know more about God. It is necessary for us to look at ourselves in the mirror of the Scriptures. We need to seek his will and look at our own lives in relationship to him.

## Putting My Life in the Proper Order

After I accepted the Lord, I attended church for two years without missing a church service. I was feeling happy. That was the place I wanted to be. I was experiencing my first love with Jesus, and the only thing I wanted to do was to stay near God. This is what happens when a person such as myself accepts Jesus Christ. We want to get completely involved in the things of the Lord.

I then decided to stay home for two years and not go to work in the mines. I found other employment closer to home so that I could spend more time with my family and my church. At that time I was already past the age of thirty. I went out to preach at any place where it might be needed. I participated in prayer vigils and other activities in the church, together with my wife and daughters. God worked on my character and on my family during that time. I came to realize that from the time I was a child, my life had been under the covering of God, under the anointing of his promise.

Those were two of the happiest years of my life. I was serving the Lord in every possible way and going out to any place that he would send me. I never lacked for anything, and it was a beautiful thing for me. But my daughters were students, and I needed to make sure we had sufficient medical insurance and could meet other expenses. We could not cover the cost unless I returned to my previous employment.

Even though our priority should not be directed to material things, God wants the best for our lives and for our children. How can we help our children if we do not have a good job? It is necessary to work to provide for food and clothing, but those things are not enough. I had to accept the situation and realize that God wanted me to be a prosperous man, someone capable of reaching another dimension in his life's work. I believe that God gave me a green light to return to my work in the mines. It was time for me to be a light

*It was time for me to be a light in my own home so that I could inspire my family to more.*

in my own home so that I could inspire my family to more.

From that time forward, in each of the cities or towns in which we went to work, the first thing I did was find a church to attend while I was there. We found good places to nourish our physical bodies, but we also looked for a church to nourish our spirits with the Word of the Lord. The Bible states, "Do not be deceived: God cannot be mocked. A man reaps what he sows" (Galatians 6:7). I loved the Lord and his work, and I recognized my need to be with God, to feel his presence, and to feel strengthened, as well as to learn from his Word.

# CHAPTER 4

## The Mountain Speaks

The San José mine is located about twenty-eight miles from the city of Copiapó in the Atacama Desert, the driest place in the world. It was developed as a copper mine by the San Esteban mining company. I had been working at that mine for about seven months, operating a huge drill mounted on a hydraulic chassis. The machine was powered by electric motors of varying sizes so that it could be used for different-size tunnels. It had advanced controls to position it precisely for the best effect.

Even though I began as a laborer, I was experienced in all the different stages of mine operations. Then I learned how to manage this huge machine and serve as chief over the laborers. Although I did not prefer giving orders, I had accepted the position because it was to be only for a short time. I decided that I should enjoy this job as a blessing of

God and made it my goal to do things productively and peacefully.

A normal work shift consisted of drilling and then clearing away the debris. Then I would move to another place and do the same thing all over again. Each drilling operation took about two hours, depending on the radius of the area to be drilled. When I finished drilling, the next worker would come and place explosives in the drilled area and detonate them. Debris would pile up there until front loaders came to gather it and take it out to the trucks.

Although the process sounds simple, this was very dangerous work. San José was a copper mine, but it was being worked as a gold mine. The copper extracted from the mine was of low quality, but the gold found there seemed to justify maintaining the mine. That is why an inappropriate practice such as overexcavating was adopted there. This practice does not produce the best results, but it was done because of human greed.

Overexcavation was not the only hazard. We were drilling at a depth of about 1,600 to 2,300 feet underground. There was nothing to extract higher than or below that point because everything was already exhausted. In addition, the mine lacked ventilation. The heat of the motors from the trucks and machinery intensifies the effect of the carbon monoxide emitted by the machinery. Added to the high temperatures of about 93 degrees Fahrenheit, it creates a very dangerous environment. I personally experienced two accidents there due to an accumulation of nitrous gases and carbon monoxide. On both occasions I passed out for at least forty minutes.

To survive these working conditions, we workers would spend our breaks in what was called "the refuge," a place with oxygen and good ventilation. We took turns going to the refuge. We would complete our tasks and then run to the refuge for oxygen.

## Dangers Ignored

I knew that working conditions in the San José mine were not good and that safety at the mine was not optimal. Every miner is well aware of what he is exposing himself to before signing a contract, but understanding the danger is not the same thing as experiencing it firsthand. Things were not being done well. Although we notified the authorities of the situation, they never paid attention to us.

Those of us with years of experience in the mining industry know that the mountain warns when something is about to happen. This has been true in all the places I have worked. Those who are in the know say, "The mine speaks." It is as if from inside its bowels the mountain begins to shout, "Be careful! I might burst. The pressures are building up to an explosion."

*The mountain warns when something is about to happen.*

The mountain had been warning us of danger for quite a while, perhaps even for months. We were beginning to hear unusual sounds and rumblings from the rocks inside the mountain. Something was happening in each of the places we walked, even in the access tunnel. There had been explosions of small rocks in the bends and at other locations. We had shared this with the chief, and the geologist had warned that the mine could collapse but that the ramp should remain intact. So he sent us back to work again, telling us to stay calm.

The truth is, they did nothing. For some owners, a spade is worth more than the life of a miner. They were only interested in maintaining production at the mine, without concern for the lives of the workers. This is why some mines are rated first-class, and others are not. We cannot categorize them all in the same way, because some mines have conscientiously adopted safety rules and procedures that should be the norm inside every mine. There are mines, and then there are mines. There are owners, and then there are owners.

The collapse of the San José mine was one of the most serious accidents in the recent history of mining in Chile. The incident has placed a glaring spotlight on the risks involved in mining and the terrible working conditions inside mines. It also serves as evidence of the lack of prevention and security measures needed to protect the lives of the miners. I personally believe that this accident occurred so that changes would be made within the mining industry to give the role of the miner its proper dignity.

## Other Warnings

During my seven months in the San José mine before the accident, I was working in shifts of seven and seven. I would spend one week at the mine and the next week at home. During my last week at home, before I left to return to the mine, something strange happened. A person who accepts Christ is sealed with the Holy Spirit, and God begins to become a perceptible reality in that person's life. That is how I began to feel God near me before I knew what was coming. Others felt him too.

My grandmother, who is still living, felt that God

was telling her that I would go through some difficult circumstances, a very dangerous and complex situation, and that it would be hard for me to leave. Based on that perception, she called my mother and shared this thought with her so that they both could pray. However, one prayer was not enough for her, and a few hours later, she called again. God sent her twice to seek prayer for me.

When my wife learned of this, she became very anxious and fearful. She was aware of the dangerous conditions at the mine because I had told her some of my concerns about it. After learning of the message from my grandmother, I said that at any moment something terrible could happen.

When I left the house, my parting from my daughter had been very different from past goodbyes. She was arguing with the taxi driver because he would not hurry. When I said farewell to her, I felt the presence of the Lord embracing us, and I thought, "Something is going to happen. I cannot explain such a close and affectionate farewell from my daughter, in contrast to past farewells that were so different, so much happier."

Later, while traveling to the mine to start the workweek, I was meditating on what my grandmother had said: "You are going to have a problem, and you will find it hard to leave." I knew from reading the Bible and meditating on it that the way of the gospel is not strewn with rose petals. Rather, as the Word teaches us, "These [trials] have come so that the proven genuineness of your faith — of greater worth than gold, which perishes even though refined by fire — may result in praise, glory and honor when Jesus Christ is revealed" (1 Peter 1:7). This tells us that our faith will be tested, not just once, but on many occasions. So I went on my way praying, "Lord, may your will be done."

## The Rocks Explode

On the night of August 4, we slept at the campground in Copiapó. The next day, August 5, was to be my first day on duty. The work shift began very early that morning, as with every morning. By the time the sun was rising on the horizon, we were already preparing for another day of hard work. We arrived at the workplace by bus, changed into appropriate work clothing, and went to our stations to get started. There we received our instructions for the day, and with each man carrying his tools, lantern, helmet, and personal items, we boarded the trucks to travel into the depths of the mine. Although our group usually entered the mine in a truck along with all the other workers, on this day we entered earlier than usual in a smaller truck. We were traveling with our boss, unhurriedly, relaxed.

He almost never came to the mine because he was not required to do so.

At the entrance to the mine, various statues depicting saints and the Virgin Mary are mounted on the rocks. Some of my work companions salute these objects as they enter the mine, while others of us pray to God when entering the tunnel. To some observers, these may seem like the same religious rituals with only a different object of superstition. But it is not the same. For some, the ritual is merely a reflex that lasts only a few seconds. Prayer, however, is a conscious act, a dialogue that often begins in our homes before we leave for work. When we pray, we feel protected and can trust our futures to the invisible God. This is a custom practiced by evangelical Christian mine workers, and it makes a difference.

*When we pray, we feel protected and can trust our futures to the invisible God.*

Upon entering the mine, we had an attitude of trust and confidence as we were prepared for the routines and responsibilities of our normal workday. Specialists in explosives enter the mine together with specialists in various types of machinery. Later come the truck drivers and those who work in the areas of security or are in charge of repairs, and finally the miners themselves go to their posts. On that day the workers entered one by one until the work shift was fully staffed with everyone ready to carry out the usual routines, just like any other workday.

Mechanics sent to repair some pieces of machinery entered the mine with me. While I was working with my team, one of them said, "Mr. José, we want you to do us a favor. We know that you will not have a lot of work to do this morning, so we want you to check this equipment and make a note of any defects you may observe. We want to know all of the problems with this item now because we will soon be taking it away for repairs." I answered affirmatively. Of course, it was my duty to do so. "We are here to work and to do whatever you need us to do," I answered.

I recall that it took me about an hour and a half to fulfill this request. I carefully inspected the machine so that they could send it to the maintenance department for repair the next day. I removed one of the wheels, which was in very bad condition, and took it to the workshop. From there, I went to the refuge.

At about two o'clock in the afternoon, we were suddenly overwhelmed by the powerful thundering of rocks. The explosion of rocks was like a rolling wave that left us covered with dirt. There was a dense cloud of dust that would take four long hours to dissipate. The human soul tends to perceive these events in terms of their own story, but the first thing we all thought to do was to stand very still for several seconds until we could get a better sense of the danger that had so abruptly interrupted our routine. We were all very concerned about what was happening under our feet, above our heads, and in the walls that seemed to be swaying around us.

We were all at different locations inside the mine, but the refuge seemed like the logical place to take shelter. Little by little, each person began to straggle in. Even though it was at a lower level inside the mine, it was the most secure place. In fact, this place was specially prepared for the type of situation we faced. Whenever a mine is built, geologists designate the most secure location as a refuge, verifying its trustworthiness by the stability of the rock formations. The refuge measured sixteen by forty-nine feet (about the size of a truck) and was to be stocked with oxygen, water, and food for crisis situations just like this one.

After the explosions of rock and the landslides ended and the cloud of dust settled, thirty-three of us were assembled in the refuge. One by one, we confirmed that none of us had sustained any injury. That, at least, was cause for celebration and filled us with a sense of wonder.

# CHAPTER 5

## Finding Refuge

mmediately after the accident, I knew that the way out of the mine was blocked. Whenever an access tunnel is abruptly cut off, the ears provide the first warning. So we had some idea of what had taken place, but we were not sure exactly what had happened.

When the dust and the smoke settled enough for us to venture out of the refuge to look around, we began to understand. The access tunnel was blocked by a huge wave of rocks and debris. We were concerned about two miners who had left the area just prior to the accident. Had they been able to get out of the mine alive? Or were they trapped somewhere in the rubble?

We conducted several inspections to search for an escape route. We tried to leave through the ventilation shafts, but that proved to be impossible. We did not have equipment such as ladders or ropes that we could use to scale vertical heights. In addition, our lanterns were damaged. To continue seeking an escape would mean exposing ourselves to additional danger. So from the first day we abandoned any hopes of an easy exit. We returned to the refuge and resigned ourselves to the fact that we had done everything humanly possible. Escape was out of the question.

We also were unable to communicate with the outside. We knew that those outside the mine assumed that if we were alive, we would be trying to take shelter in the refuge. We were, in fact, in the refuge, but our inability to show that we were alive and well weighed on our minds.

After the understanding that we had no escape route sank in, we discussed the situation among ourselves. We needed to organize ourselves for a new and different lifestyle in order to survive until rescuers arrived. We had no idea how long that might take. And so our struggle to survive began.

## Assessing Our Situation

The machine that I operated, the Jumbo, was located very near the ventilation shaft. When I saw it, I realized that if it had not been for the damaged wheel, I would have been at my post operating the machine that was now completely buried under the rocks! My coworkers, together with the boss, were farther away from the ventilation shaft, so they were able to run away from the area that caved in. But if I had been operating the machine at the time, the shower of rocks and debris likely would have ended my life and I would not be telling this story. Just the thought of this small detail gave me a sense of assurance that God was protecting me.

Not everyone in the group had this sense of assurance, however. Each person's character was different, and not everyone in the group reacted in the same way. Not all of us were veterans. Our group included both men who were very young and new to mining — some with only four to six days of experience on the job — and men who were much older and had many years of experience and knowledge about the mining industry. Nevertheless, we generally maintained very positive attitudes about our situation, even though we had to recognize that as mere men there was nothing we could do to save ourselves.

The conditions we faced tested all of us. The refuge did not have adequate ventilation, so the temperature was 89 to 93 degrees Fahrenheit all the time. All the electrical controls that had formerly powered the ventilation fans were broken, as were the conduits that supplied water and electricity. Without any way to get air circulating in the room, we all sweated profusely.

As for food, the refuge should have been stocked with enough provisions to allow for normal meal portions for several days. However, the box used to warehouse these emergency supplies contained only a few cans of tuna, salmon, and condensed milk. Even these could not be safely consumed because the expiration date was past. There were also a few packages of cookies, but those disappeared before we knew it.

As for water, the refuge should have had enough drinking water for the number of people working the average shift — in this case, thirty-three miners. The cloud of dust had left us very thirsty, so the container holding about ten and a half gallons of potable water disappeared the first day. After that, all we had left for drinking was the water we used for work purposes, which was stored in large drums. This was industrial water that was not considered potable, but it is what we drank.

Faced with these harsh realities, we decided that we would have to organize ourselves with the idea that we would be in the mine for several more days. That was the point when differing opinions were expressed. Some clamored for certain things, while others wanted to maintain the peace at any cost. Some maintained a positive attitude, while others became very negative.

Nevertheless, we set to work. We inventoried the supplies we would have available during the days ahead. We also decided that we could not all stay in one place. The refuge was too small for all of us to fit in comfortably. Besides, the heat in the refuge was becoming too intense. So we agreed to split up into three groups. One group would stay in the refuge, and the others would stay in areas higher in the mine. Next we selected and made repairs to the other areas of the mine where we could wait. This was one way we tried to make our stay underground a little more comfortable and pleasant.

We took batteries and lightbulbs out of the machines to light our newfound quarters. We used another Jumbo machine to charge the batteries because it was the most economical of all the machinery in terms of energy consumption, and we needed to carefully preserve what fuel we still had. A battery charge lasted about ten to twelve hours.

Everyone collaborated in the work effort. Each man dutifully fulfilled his assigned task in the interests of labor distribution, and this demonstrated that everyone had a good attitude. But there was one more thing that we all realized was needed—and it was not a matter of manual labor. We needed spiritual help for our souls because in this terrible situation fear was quickly taking root deep in our hearts. We understood all too well the dangers of being trapped in the depths of a mine.

## Discovering Miner Number Thirty-Four

In the shadowy darkness of that mine, it became crystal clear that God was our only hope, our only resource. I shared this thought with my friends in a conversation early in our ordeal, at a point before we began to organize ourselves and decide how we would deal with the situation. At that time they told me, "Mr. José, we want you to lead us in prayer." There was no doubt that we needed supernatural help.

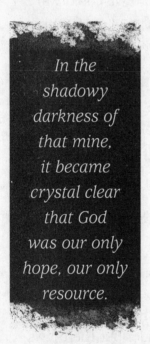

*In the shadowy darkness of that mine, it became crystal clear that God was our only hope, our only resource.*

That is how it came about that, along with other tasks, a spiritual role was delegated to me. It was not by decree or by a vote of the majority. My reputation among the men as a Christian and someone who often spoke to them about principles made me the natural choice. That is how my job as prayer leader began. My coworkers wanted me to organize a communal prayer to the Lord, unanimously asking him to free us if that was his will.

I agreed to guide them, but I told them that we Christians pray to a living God who has ears to hear and does hear us when we pray. So it would be necessary for them to pray with faith, to cry out to God in the confidence and knowledge that he hears us. If they could not pray with faith, they would have to find someone else to be their guide. And they did not refuse. They accepted my conditions and said, "We will do as you say."

The first reaction of any Christian when encountering a difficult situation should be to pray, "Lord, I am your child. Cover me with your precious blood." I can assure you that from the first day of the mining accident we began to pray. We cried out to God, and he responded. He did not need to find doors to enter that place with us, because, as we all know, "What is impossible with man is possible with God" (Luke 18:27). When we humbled ourselves in prayer before God, we felt his presence in our midst. He was there! Without a doubt, he was our thirty-fourth companion.

During the days that followed, we began to pray together, and I proclaimed the Word of God. In my preaching, I presented Christ to them, and then, without appealing to creeds or religious affiliations, we prayed in the hope of getting an answer from the Lord. I told the men, "Prayer is a conversation with the Lord, in contrast with something that is repetitive and rehearsed." I added, "Conversation with God is very important, because it is like talking to a very important person or like talking to your father when you were young and you needed something. In prayer we communicate with someone we cannot see. Nevertheless, in reality, those of us who have accepted the Lord, we who have known him, have the security of knowing that he is there because we know that his promises are true."

Prayer began to be our main source of support, and the members of the group were becoming more interested and involved because of these times of communion with God. We began to say personal prayers so that everyone could participate in a conversation with God, each in his own words. Everyone had the opportunity to praise God, to express something in his own way. Above all, our prayers had one thought in common: May God take dominion of this entire situation, because we cannot count on anyone else to hear us.

# Growing in the Word and in Knowledge of the Lord

When our confinement began, we did not have a Bible. But as I began to talk with my companions about the Lord, I found that many Bible verses and spiritual reflections I had learned earlier in my life were coming back into my memory. Each passage of the Word and parable of the Lord that I shared had been sown first in my heart. I came to realize that something the Bible teaches about Christians was happening in my life: "You show that you are a letter from Christ, the result of our ministry, written not with ink but with the Spirit of the living God, not on tablets of stone but on tablets of human hearts" (2 Corinthians 3:3).

Even though I had participated in Bible studies and had assisted at the church I had attended as a child, I had no idea that so much had been retained in my memory! Perhaps the enemy sows doubts in us because he does not want us to be interested in knowing the Word or learning more about it. However, when the moment of need comes, everything that we have heard and learned for years comes to our minds in order to edify us when we have no other way of receiving the Word.

As I took hold of what I had learned and began

to talk to my companions about the Lord, God began to work in them and gave them an opportunity to know him and communicate with him. Some of them were immediately brought out of darkness, and with great joy I saw how the Lord was transforming their lives.

One member of our group distinguished himself as the one who was to become my assistant, a "Timothy" that the Lord raised up in that darkness to be a companion so that I was not alone in my spiritual duty. I noticed him almost immediately after we started praying. He always affirmed the prayers with a "Yes, Lord. Amen, Lord. May it be so!" On the third day of our confinement, the Lord touched him, and this man took a step forward, directing these words to God in prayer: "Lord, I knew you. Please forgive me for leaving you. If you take me out of this place, I promise that I will serve you for the rest of my life."

Something marvelous occurred at that moment. I approached my coworker and gave him the opportunity to lead a general prayer and raised the possibility of his sharing with the others what the Word of God had placed in his heart. I remembered that in the prayer vigils in which I had participated as a child, people always had an opportunity to praise and glorify God. In our situation, we needed to offer these opportunities so that we could build up confidence within the group. We desired that everyone would gather around, not only to observe, but to participate and express love for God by means of personal prayer. I wanted everyone in the mine to have the opportunity to say, "Thank you, Lord" — or at least to sing his praises.

Prayer was the star player in our story. Humanly speaking, there was nothing we could do. We had no idea what was going on out-side the mine, just as the rescue workers outside had no idea what was going on inside the mine. But by means of prayer, we began to feel surrounded by the presence of the Lord. Miner number thirty-four was with us. We could feel his presence, and we talked to him daily. This is how we rose above and persevered in those days of desperate waiting when we did not know whether anyone was looking for us or whether everyone had already given us up for dead.

*Prayer was the star player in our story.*

# CHAPTER 6

## Clinging to Hope against All Odds

We stubbornly held on to hope even while we were trapped inside the dark interior of the mine. However, we were not aware of how hopeless our situation appeared to be from outside the mine. After our rescue, I read a few articles from the local newspaper *El Mundo* and other media outlets, and I now recognize anew that our situation was not good. Rescuers were faced with some very difficult circumstances. Clearly our situation was very precarious. One report read as follows:

> Monday, August 16, inside the San José mine, in the Atacama Desert — Engineers, rescue workers, and specialists from the "Chuki" and "La Andina" mining companies are competing to see who will be the first to find the thirty-three miners trapped in the bowels of the limestone mountain.

A sounding team has been working for days, and they have drilled a half-kilometer below the surface. Meanwhile, Igor, a mining engineer from northern Chile, is climbing down into the collapsed San José mine. By his side are some of the most experienced, expert miners from Chile, Peru, and Bolivia.

They hope to find the trapped miners before their coworkers, the drilling team, reach the refuge where it is thought the miners may be found. The refuge is located about 680 meters below. Igor and his team lower themselves into the mine and find a major surprise.

Sunday marked a day before and a day after in the rescue of the thirty-three miners. "We entered the mine and saw a Dantesque panorama. Everything had collapsed, and a wall made it impossible for us to continue, so we had to continue walking along a wide road. On one side was the wall, and on the other a gigantic hole. Then the ground began to crumble next to the wall so we had to jump back," Igor explains.

The dangerous condition of the work site forced the suspension of rescue operations inside the mine. "I hope that my coworkers are well, but the conditions down there must be extremely difficult," said one mining engineer.

"There are a lot of rumors about the salvage operation. Those who went in on the first day and got to within about 150 meters of the refuge said they did not find any smashed truck. They saw no cadavers, nor did they hear any noise at all," he said. "We need to be realistic. Conditions inside the mind are very bad. In my opinion, it would be hard for anyone to still be alive in there," said a specialist whose supervisors have ordered him to return to his normal workplace because there is nothing else he can do inside the San José mine.

The expert believes there are two factors directly influencing the possibility that any of the miners may still be alive. First, they did not find an "air bash" effect. "The collapsed area on the surface fills a space that, when it falls, is transformed into air that circulates at high speeds. This wind is strong enough to displace trucks, equipment, and people as if they were feathers," he said. "The lower part of the mine is divided into two parts. We are certain that there were people working in the production areas. We hope that the 'air bash' did not reach the area where they were located," Igor said.

The other big problem is the element of liquid. Igor believes that there is no water in the mine. "The only water that they may have is industrial water used for operations. It is not potable water, but in these circumstances it would not matter. The water pipes were completely torn out in the collapse. The only other possibility would be if some puddle had formed and they had found it. We should keep in mind that they were working in temperatures 38 degrees Centigrade [about 100 degrees Fahrenheit], which is why the risk of dehydration is very high."

Igor adds that this mine did not really have a refuge as such. "The poorest refuges are rocky formations that are hermetically sealed to protect against fires. They should be stocked with food and oxygen machines. The San José mine did not have any of that."

The other thing that worries Igor is the silence that the first rescue workers heard when they almost reached the refuge on Sunday, two days after the accident. "They did not hear anything, which means that they are hermetically sealed," he explained. "If there were some way for air to get in, fine. If not, they will consume the air they have until they start falling into a deep sleep," he added. According to Igor, at any moment there could be another collapse, perhaps even larger than the one that left the thirty-three miners trapped inside. "Of course, they have cordoned off the area because we are afraid that the entire San José mine may collapse due to the 'sweeping effect,'" he said.

"In any case, the miners are experts. We hope that they were capable of dealing with the circumstances and will soon be with us again," the engineer concludes before leaving the hotel Terrasol de Caldera. Tomorrow will be the thirteenth day since the accident occurred.

Perhaps it is just as well that we did not know what the assessment was from the outside. Inside the mine, not even the most incredulous unbeliever could deny that something supernatural was happening. God was strengthening us in hope, in spirit, in confidence, and in unity. Our prayer — the cry of our hearts — was for unity, so that we would all be rowing the boat in the same direction. And that is what God did.

We were becoming a society with a common goal and shared values. We were experiencing a unity of emotion and thought that we Christians call "communion." Although it is normal for a large group of diverse people to have disagreements when experiencing situations such as ours, we had very few disagreements among ourselves. Down there, a different spirit had taken hold of each one of the men. We could feel that spirit moving among us when we prayed. As we prayed, we became more and more confident of the certainty that God would rescue us.

## Our Hope Is Tested

Obviously some of the men, as my father used to say, "did not commune with us." Not all of them were willing to accept the lordship of Christ and humble themselves before God. Yet we continued to see the power of God manifested in mighty ways. We saw very powerful demonstrations that the Holy Spirit was present there. We even saw the Holy Spirit resting on us in the form of a dove.

To have this type of vision was marvelous for those who believe. However, for those who do not believe, the Bible says it will be foolishness: "The person without the Spirit does not accept the things that come from the Spirit of God but considers them foolishness, and cannot understand them because they are discerned only through the Spirit" (1 Corinthians 2:14). So for some of the men, hearing about these things and seeing another miner crying out to the Lord with all of his heart, with tears running down his cheeks, produced resistance.

The world does not and cannot fully understand what we were experiencing down below. Explaining our reason for hope is complicated. To a man whose confidence is in his own strength, the gospel will be foolishness. But God shows his children things when it is imperative — when it is important for us and when it serves his purpose. I had hope because I understood the words of my grandmother to be a sign from the one who knows with precision, beforehand, everything that will occur.

Even when we walk in faith before the Lord, the Bible affirms that the Lord tests his own. As children of God, we often are tested like gold in the refiner's fire. These are the inscrutable mysteries of God. It is amazing the way that he does these things. In the mine, we certainly faced tests and opportunities for discouragement, many times when we could have lost hope.

From the day of the accident we did not know anything about what was happening outside the mine. We knew nothing of our wives, fathers, mothers, siblings, and children. We knew nothing of any attempt to rescue us.

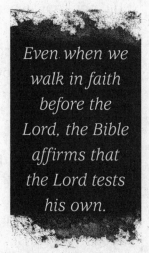

*Even when we walk in faith before the Lord, the Bible affirms that the Lord tests his own.*

Eventually we heard drilling in the rocks. They were using a sounding drill to try to reach us!

A sounding drill has a tube in the middle through which we would be able to communicate with those outside the mine. This was an encouraging sign, a tangible reason for hope.

As we listened, however, we realized that the sounds of the drill were no longer coming from above. Instead, we heard noises below us. The sounding drill had gone off target! It had not reached the refuge. It had missed us by some distance and passed us by. With it went the hopes of many.

## Relying on a Living Hope

With heavy-hearted frustration, we realized that there would not be many more such attempts. We did not know when those on the surface might call a halt to their efforts to rescue us. Although this caused great discouragement among some of the men, God had shown me that he would rescue us. I believed with all my heart that our prayer had been answered long before. At that moment my thought was, "How good it is to be a child of God! How good it is to belong to the people of God and to be part of his family!"

I knew without a doubt that I was under the protection of Christ. When we surrender our lives to Jesus, in addition to being sealed by his Holy Spirit, we receive the pledge of the Holy Spirit: "Now the one who has fashioned us for this very purpose is God, who has given us the Spirit as a deposit, guaranteeing what is to come" (2 Corinthians 5:5). These promises are true, and they are activated whenever necessary.

So even at the times when the men's confidence wavered, we always had a living hope that we would leave the mine and return to our homes. We sought to demonstrate our confidence in this thought in many ways. For example, some would say, "I am certain that I will get out," or "I am not going to let the devil trick me," or "I want to live." During the entire time we spent inside the mine, we continued to pray daily, without fail. Several times we held prayer meetings twice a day — at noon and later at six o'clock in the evening.

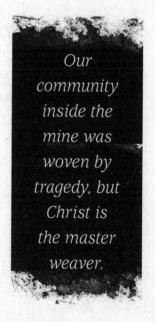

*Our community inside the mine was woven by tragedy, but Christ is the master weaver.*

Our community inside the mine was woven by tragedy, but Christ is the master weaver. We sought in every way to live in the unity, community, and hope he provides. We sought to do this even when we disagreed. Following one heated discussion between people who were good friends, a time of prayer took place, and they shook hands, embraced, and asked each other for forgiveness. Their friendship was immediately restored.

"This is not a place to be at odds with one another," I would tell them. "The Lord likes to add and multiply, not divide. Besides, we cannot be divided here, so please let us put an end to this matter and send the devil on down below where he belongs, because he cannot stay here." It may sound strange to say, "Send the devil below," from a location 2,300 feet underground, but you can be certain that in any location you find yourself on this earth, hostilities and challenges will come from below. If you keep your eyes on the hope of heaven, whether or not you can see with your physical eyes, sooner or later help will arrive.

# CHAPTER 7

## We Are Well
## in the Refuge

t is not enough for a Christian to know the Bible. The Word teaches us that we must also put it into practice: "If I speak in the tongues of men or of angels, but do not have love, I am only a resounding gong or a clanging cymbal" (1 Corinthians 13:1). So I believe it is necessary for a Christian to be humble, simple, friendly, loving, and affectionate rather than subdued, serious, and distant, as some believe they ought to be. I want to try to reach people, to seek their friendship so that I know what is happening with them and how to help them. I don't want to be an impenetrable wall. I want to socialize and enjoy the company of others and demonstrate that a Christian is friendly, generous, and warm.

My place is to be with people, and the mine became the precise and precious place to speak about Christ and demonstrate the love and hope that only he can give. But the task certainly wasn't easy. Among the thirty-three, there was a great diversity of personalities and experience. We did not start out as a cohesive group.

On the job, each man focused on doing his duty, and we did not have close relationships with each other. Some of us had been sent in by an outside consulting business, so we were at the mine temporarily merely to fulfill our specific work duties and nothing more. We would report only to the manager or other chief on duty, but there was little, if any, interaction with our coworkers. Other workers lived nearby and belonged to the permanent workforce of the company.

Some of the men were young and inexperienced, possessing little knowledge of mines, while others were older and had spent most of their lives working under the earth. During the first days, the young men especially seemed a little sad due to a lack of confidence. There were also moments and situations when they used certain unpleasant words, even though sometimes they were said in jest. In any case, they were impetuous and said things at inappropriate times. It seemed that they felt misunderstood, and their attitude was not positive. I felt directed to approach them in order to encourage them and to show myself as a caring friend.

With the passing days, the attitudes of those

young men began to change. They began to show many positive qualities and do many good things. Some of them distinguished themselves, which is worthy of mention because even though they were young and did not have a lot of experience, they behaved like men. They were also sensitive to the things of God and sought a closer relationship with the Lord.

After our first seventeen days together under those terrible living conditions, the thirty-three of us became well acquainted. The relationships between most of the men became much closer. Even though some of the miners said little, we spoke with one another about our lives in a deep way. We became more united and worked as a single team.

## Enjoying a Feast before the Lord

We might not have had the décor or the musical instruments that one normally sees in a church, but before we knew it, the refuge had become a church. Having found ourselves 2,300 feet underground, we were present, seeking God with sincere hearts, united in one accord in our praise to him. And each day we were trapped inside the mine we experienced the presence of "Miner Thirty-Four,"

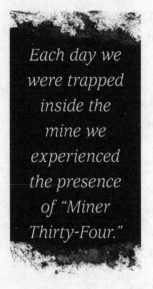

*Each day we were trapped inside the mine we experienced the presence of "Miner Thirty-Four."*

as we called him. Each day God filled us with strength and joy.

Imagine that! We prayed and sang praises to God while we were facing death, and I believe that God was pleased with us because of it. Daily we observed extraordinary things. For example, one of the men was feeling very ill, and his body was becoming weak. So we anointed him in the name of the Lord, and the following day he was feeling well and ready to resume his duties.

We also pleaded with God continually to take away our hunger, to multiply our food, and to add more nutrition to it. God answered by satisfying our hunger. This alone was an amazing miracle because we had so little. The food we had would only have lasted about three or four days if we had consumed normal meal portions, and we lived on it for seventeen days!

It wasn't easy. We knew by experience that we could be inside the mine for many more days, so we had to divide the little bit we had into smaller portions so that the supplies would last longer. When even these ran low, we began to fast — first for twenty-four hours, later for forty-eight hours, and finally for seventy-two hours — in order to allow plenty of time for the people working above to reach us.

The severe fasting caused some conflicts. Nevertheless, everyone understood our situation. We had to accept the fact that we were racing against death and that we needed to be strong and courageous. Besides, we had agreed to organize ourselves into a democratic system, and the opinion of the majority was what counted. No one gave orders. All of our decisions were made in concert, supported by prayer. We discovered that a democracy supported by prayer is an excellent system that produces very good results.

We established a fixed schedule for mealtimes. Each time we were scheduled to eat, we asked for God's blessing on our meager resources. We took turns praying and giving thanks for the food before each meal. For some of our coworkers, this was quite a novelty. Finally all we had left was one can of tuna, about a cup and a half.

As we were about to consume our last bit of food, we decided to serve the meal in a different way. We decided to celebrate what we called "the last supper," even though it was during the lunch hour. We left the refuge and went into an area of the mine that had been more affected by the collapse. We chose this location because more air was circulating there, and we wanted to light a fire and heat a pan of water to make a hot meal. Each man then placed his portion of tuna in the pan, and we made a tuna soup. If we had eaten the tuna dry, each of us would have eaten about half a tablespoon, but because we shared our portions, each of us enjoyed a cup of hot "tuna soup." The broth gave us a hot meal that we could savor and take a longer time to consume.

The delicious aroma while the soup was cooking excited all of us. We thought that perhaps the smoke from the cooking fire would go out through the one ventilation shaft that was left and serve as a signal to the rescue workers. Later, the rescuers said they had seen the smoke, but it did not occur to them that it was coming from us.

After eating the soup, some of the men lay down for a siesta, just as if we had enjoyed a good roast beef dinner. I also lay down to rest for a little while and to see if I could manage to sleep, but I could not. I remained awake. While I was lying there, I had a vision. It was a very vivid impression of struggling against the enemy of my soul. I was fighting a battle in which he wanted to knock me down, but he was not able.

In the vision, two worldly spirits were speaking to me. The first tried to overwhelm me with fear. The other said, "Take me." As I reflected on these things, I gave thanks to the Lord. I understood that even the demons knew that God would take us out of there! And they also wanted to leave that place.

I got up from this experience and was filled with joy. I walked toward the refuge, glorifying God for the confirmation that we would soon be outside. For me that was something tremendous. I did not tire of giving him thanks.

> *I can affirm with all my heart that the Lord is the one who strengthens us.*

Even today I thank God for the vision that I had while awake. I can affirm with all my heart that the Lord is the one who strengthens us. He is the source of all strength. God provides us with everything through prayer and his Holy Spirit.

## The Drill Breaks Through!

God wants to see a change of attitude in people. He wants us to set aside our pride, our self-esteem, and our self-sufficiency. God wants us to be who we really are, to realize that we are nothing but a fistful of dust to which the Lord gave the breath of life. I think that during our most desperate time in the mine, we touched the heart of God with our attitude and our faith. I believe that the Lord showed us the place where we should go because he knew where the second probing drill would hit.

Our joy was complete when, after seventeen days of waiting, the second sounding drill finally reached the refuge. It was, and was not, a surprise. We waited, listened, and watched in the refuge until we knew that the drill was about to break through. We prepared to act rapidly the moment the drill entered the room. The people on the surface must know that we were well and that the refuge was the place where we could be found.

When the sounding drill broke through, we signaled that we were there by striking the iron drill mechanism with a hammer so that it would vibrate outside. After the operators above felt the vibrations, they stopped the machine. This gave us time to attach the messages we had prepared and also to paint the iron drill in such a way that they would notice an unusual mark. We had more than enough time to tie the messages to the sounding drill and apply the paint.

As a miner, I know how to locate the path of the tunnel that is being drilled, and when I saw the point where the drill had entered the refuge, I was very glad. It was exactly the place where the Lord had shown me it would come. Now we only needed to wait for the men above to do their job. It was only a matter of time. The miracle had occurred.

After seventeen days of being trapped 2,300 feet underground, we had finally made contact with the outside world! The sounding drill brought us renewed hope. The world above had not abandoned us. They knew that we were alive. Our families were outside waiting, and what God had shown me began to be fulfilled.

We were jubilant. Our joy was unspeakable. Our celebration down below was crazy. No news was released to the country, however, until the president of Chile, Sebastián Piñera, arrived at the mine.

Of several messages sent to the surface that day, the one that was publicized to the world was written by a coworker in thick blue marker: "We are well in the refuge, the 33." Thus began the communication between us and the outside and between the outside and us. Because the celebration was going on at both ends of the chasm, that distance seemed so much smaller.

# The World Breaks In to Our Refuge

The arrival of the drill brought changes for our group. It would be many more days before the final rescue would take place. The rescuers already knew that from the time they initially discovered that we were alive until the capsule would be ready to extract us from the mine, we would have to spend many days waiting and being patient. For that reason, their number one priority was to strengthen us and keep us calm.

The first step was to survey the area and select a good place to make a larger opening several feet from the first in order to supply us with food and water. For the first four days they gave us only water with sugar. Even though we really wanted a steak dinner, we understood that this was the right thing to do to prepare our bodies for solid food.

We were assigned a team of psychologists who started to treat us like children, not like men. I believe they thought that we were not lucid, that we were in a dreadful mental condition. However, they were in for a big surprise. After only a few conversations with the people outside, they realized that we were sane, that we reasoned with clarity of mind, and that we were in good spirits. No one could believe it! Stomach ailments were the only problem that some of us had, but mentally we were all well. Eventually they had to replace the psychologist in charge of the team because none of us would talk to him.

We also began to communicate with our families and to exchange letters. One of our first questions to the outside world was about the two coworkers who had left the mine shortly before its collapse. We did not know what had happened to them, and we thought they might have been trapped in the rubble. Thankfully they had gotten out. Knowing they were safe was one less concern for us. We were happy to know that all the miners were well, both above and below.

After the rescuers began sending us food, we also received many gifts. One of those gifts was Bibles, one for each of the thirty-three men trapped in the mine. We were very surprised to see that the Bible Society of Chile, which had donated the Bibles, had engraved them with the name of each of the miners, along with the following message: "Good books should be in good hands." It was a great blessing for each of us to have a copy of the Word of God to read, enabling us to more actively participate in the Bible study we held during our prayer meetings. We each also received an audio recording of the Bible, done in theatrical style. These things made the Word much easier to understand,

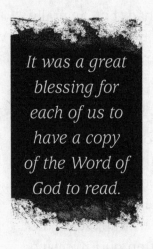

*It was a great blessing for each of us to have a copy of the Word of God to read.*

and the young men liked it very much.

However, we also began to receive a variety of religious items that people wanted to have rubbed on the walls of the refuge. They sensed that a miracle had occurred there, and they believed that the power in that place could be transferred onto the items. Such ignorance! The Scriptures clearly state, "You shall not make for yourself an image in the form of anything in heaven above or on the earth beneath or in the waters below" (Exodus 20:4). Yes, it is true that a miracle took place down below, but it was because a group of men cried out to the Lord and humbled themselves before God — and he in his great mercy answered their prayers.

Other things were sent down into the mine that we never should have received. People provided us with pornographic magazines and reading materials full of dirty jokes. They thought these things would be good and would help the men stay happy. But none of us had asked for them, and they were not good. They definitely corrupted the atmosphere. Sadly, such things represent the hollow happiness that the world offers.

Whenever I look back and think about those difficult days that we lived through, I am amazed by the miracle that God accomplished. One of the engineers in charge of the rescue later said that the second sounding drill that finally reached us had gone off track — a deviation for which there is no technical explanation. This reminds me that *only God* had the power to change its path. Never before had a drill gone off target in that way. And therein lies the miracle. If it had gone a foot or two to one side, it would have passed us by again. Instead the second drill hit the vertex, right on the "equator." It entered exactly where it should. God does everything to perfection.

Yes, I remember the hardships and isolation. I remember the sadness that overwhelmed us when the first sounding drill passed us by. I also remember the day that we ran out of food, and how we prayed that the Lord would multiply that last ration and provide for us. How quickly God answered our prayer! After the second probe broke through, the box of food was never empty again. The times of prayer in our underground refuge kept us united and confident. But God deserves all the credit for saving us. He kept us well in the refuge.

# CHAPTER 8

## Salvation Draws Near

One of the hardest lessons we learned in the depths of the mine was how to stay patient and to bear with each other. Even though I thought of myself as a patient man, and I had experience in working alongside different kinds of people, I learned not just to tolerate other people but to accept them as they are. I know and understand personally how hard it can be to get along with other people, especially to accept others with whom we have differences. On one occasion at the El Indio mine, another miner had said of me, "Let's call on the evangelical

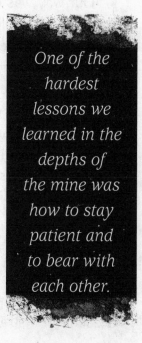

*One of the hardest lessons we learned in the depths of the mine was how to stay patient and to bear with each other.*

man for a little laugh." It can be a challenge to work with different kinds of personalities, to converse with respect and an attitude of acceptance, and to seek reconciliation.

We had a great deal of work to do to prepare for our rescue, which provided many opportunities to exercise patience, wisdom, and understanding. To begin with, the psychologists and other personnel outside the mine were sending directions about how we should organize ourselves inside the mine. After a while, we finally told them that their way would not work and that we would do it our way.

Our way was to organize in three groups, each with eleven people, so that we could cover the task of distributing the supplies that were arriving from the outside around the clock. Items sent down to us had to be squeezed into a very small space, making it necessary to organize them upon receipt, and in some cases to assemble items, such as the cots they sent us for sleeping. Each of us had our assigned tasks, and because we all had good attitudes, good spirits, and renewed hope, the work environment was very good.

One of our early tasks was to remove the rock on our end of the new tunnel the rescuers were drilling so that the rescue capsule could safely descend in a straight line. The shift foreman who was with us played a very important role in that job. He and the manager took measurements and sent the reference points to the engineers who were outside, so that they would not be drilling blindly.

During the new stage of waiting, we endeavored to be patient in regard to the distribution of food, which was sometimes a point of concern. Although we were receiving enough food, everything had to be distributed in an equitable way so as to "keep the peace" and ensure that each man received his designated meal portion. The same thing was true of water rations. Finally the box began to fill up with food, bottled water, and even desserts.

## Living between Two Worlds

During the weeks of waiting, I slept little and drank a lot of coffee to keep myself awake. Because of my work duties, the time I needed to prepare messages, the prayer meetings, and other tasks, my schedule was often disrupted. Even now, many months later, my sleep is still altered.

Whenever I was fulfilling my assigned duties, carrying out some activity, or resting, my assistant, "Timothy," would take my place. However, my greatest concern was to start the prayer times promptly at noon and at six o'clock in the evening. I knew that if I was not there, the prayer time might be called off or some confusion might take place. For this reason, we agreed to stop everything at noon — regardless of what we were doing — and gather to pray before returning to our duties. We also took advantage of our new communications with the outside world to organize a prayer chain with the Christians in the campground who were in charge of our rescue.

Although our communication with the outside brought many advantages, it was also difficult. Unlike some, I hesitated to communicate with my wife and my daughters because I knew it would greatly affect my emotions. I did not even want them to be outside in the campground waiting for me to come out. Nevertheless, they are adults, and they made their own decisions. Later I learned that my daughters stayed at the campground from the first day of our discovery, as did my nephews and nieces, siblings, in-laws, and the rest of the family.

My first contact by videoconference was with one of my daughters. It was not easy to talk, but it was very exciting for me. During our conversation I could see the sun shining in the sky in the video image. That little hint of blue sky made me want to hurry and get out as soon as possible. However, I had to be content and wait patiently. I found that writing letters was the most comfortable way of expressing myself and communicating with my family.

## A Call to Salvation

The rescue workers were starting to make significant progress, hammering on the rocks night and day. It was not easy to live with the constant noise, and one day we were covered by a great cloud of dust. But we did not complain. The alternative would have been for our rescuers to stop drilling, so we preferred to endure to the end.

When I realized that it would not be long before we would be leaving, I felt that I should make a call during our time of prayer for the men to accept the Lord. For weeks we had faithfully preached the gospel, planting the seed of faith. We had witnessed all that God had done for us. We had prayed for the sick and even prayed for requests we received from the outside. Our meetings were not just prayer times but complete church services. The young men continued to be enthusiastic about our spiritual activities. They dared to pray and also to sing. They took charge of distributing the folders that contained the lyrics of the songs we sang. We sang familiar hymns such as "Onward Christian Soldiers" and "I Live, Lord, Because You Live."

Now all that was left for them to do was to take a step of faith and accept into their hearts the God who had been with them all along. This was something that I could have led them through myself, but I thought it would be good to have a local pastor participate in the meeting by videoconference. I had been privileged to help them to trust in God and to get through those difficult days with faith and hope, but I needed to be sure that someone would continue the task after we had left the mine. I was thinking of their spiritual growth and ongoing need for discipleship. So I called on a pastor from Copiapó — the nearest city, the one in which most of the men lived. He would be able to follow up with the men after we were on the outside.

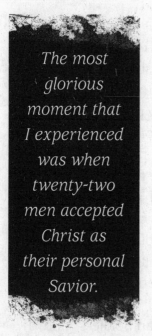

*The most glorious moment that I experienced was when twenty-two men accepted Christ as their personal Savior.*

On a Sunday, during the noonday prayer meeting, the pastor said a few words, and we sang some praise songs. Then he offered a prayer that included the call to salvation. Twenty-two of the thirty-three miners trapped in the depths of the mine made a personal commitment to the Lord and said, "Yes, I accept Christ." I glorify

God for the life of this servant who served as Christ's representative when Christ received my coworkers and wrote their names in the Book of Life.

Today I can affirm that during those days inside the mine, while trapped by those huge boulders 2,300 feet underground, the most glorious moment that I experienced was when twenty-two men accepted Christ as their personal Savior. My heart's cry is that everyone would come to accept the Lord without waiting for a time until hardships and difficulties come. We do not need to be 2,300 feet under the earth and trapped for sixty-nine days to experience God. But sometimes we are so hardheaded that only when we are facing difficult circumstances will we look toward heaven and find our true salvation.

# CHAPTER 9

## Thank You, Lord!

During the final days before the arrival of the capsule, the team on the outside told us about an idea suggested by a missionary who works with a worldwide ministry that helps young people. He explained that it would be extraordinary if each one of the miners came out of the mine wearing a shirt that says, "Thank you, Lord!" Considering that the television cameras of the entire world would be recording every detail of what was happening at that moment, this would be a unique opportunity to tell the world that the men who had been trapped inside the mine had experienced a personal encounter with God. It would be a way of showing our gratitude to God and letting the whole planet know that God answers the prayers of those who cry out to him.

Before accepting this proposal, I spoke with my coworkers because all of our decisions were made in a democratic way. I brought up the subject at one of our noonday prayer meetings, explaining that if we accepted the suggestion, it would be a practical way of testifying about the Lord. Also, if we wore those shirts, we would not even need to open our mouths. The slogan on the front would read, "Thank you, Lord!" in English and in Spanish. This Scripture verse would be engraved on the back of the shirt: "In his hand are the depths of the earth, and the mountain peaks belong to him" (Psalm 95:4).

Later in our meeting we read the entire psalm:

Come, let us sing for joy to the LORD;
    let us shout aloud to the Rock of our salvation.
Let us come before him with thanksgiving
    and extol him with music and song.

For the LORD is the great God,
    the great King above all gods.
In his hand are the depths of the earth,
    and the mountain peaks belong to him.
The sea is his, for he made it,
    and his hands formed the dry land.

Come, let us bow down in worship,
    let us kneel before the LORD our Maker;
for he is our God
    and we are the people of his pasture,
    the flock under his care.

Today, if only you would hear his voice,
"Do not harden your hearts as you did at
    Meribah,
    as you did that day at Massah in the
    wilderness,
where your ancestors tested me;
    they tried me, though they had seen what
      I did.
For forty years I was angry with that generation;
    I said, 'They are a people whose hearts go
      astray,
    and they have not known my ways.'
So I declared on oath in my anger,
    'They shall never enter my rest.' "

No one in the group expressed any opposition to accepting the proposal, so a few days later they sent the shirts. At first I thought I would wait to give them to the men, one by one, as they were leaving. However, I also knew they were men of their word and would fulfill the commitment they had made. The truth is that not all of the men put on their shirts before getting into the capsule. Some of them had already sent their shirts to the surface along with their personal belongings, but they were a minority. All in all, the important thing is that the world saw, read, and discussed what was seen on those shirts.

# October 13, 2010

As the hours passed and the time of our rescue drew near, our expectations grew. The men were getting more and more anxious about leaving. For several days, we wondered if the tunnel they had drilled was wide enough to get us to the surface. However, the Word tells us, "Now faith is confidence in what we hope for and assurance about what we do not see" (Hebrews 11:1). We decided to trust that God would provide a way to get us out of there. We clearly understood that what is impossible for man is possible for God. I was convinced that even if it might be impossible for men to get us out of the mine, God would do whatever was necessary to find a way.

> *I was convinced that even if it might be impossible for men to get us out of the mine, God would do whatever was necessary to find a way.*

When the capsule finally appeared, I felt overflowing joy at witnessing the Lord's answer. Immediately, the first rescue worker emerged from the capsule to greet us and then began to organize us and give us instructions about how the departure operation would work.

Those responsible for the rescue operation decided to divide us into three groups. The five most physically fit people would go first; then the eleven weakest men would be taken out, and finally the seventeen strongest men would be able to leave. According to the list provided by the government and family members, this is the order for the rescue of the thirty-three miners:

1. **Florencio Ávalos**, 31, manager
2. **Mario Sepúlveda**, 39, electrician
3. **Juan Illanes**, 52, mine worker
4. **Carlos Mamani**, 23, Bolivian machine operator
5. **Jimmy Sánchez**, 19, mine worker
6. **Osmán Araya**, 30 mine worker
7. **José Ojeda**, 46, driller
8. **Claudio Yañez**, 34, drill operator
9. **Mario Gómez**, 63, mine worker
10. **Álex Vega**, 31, mechanic
11. **Jorge Galleguillos**, 56, mine worker
12. **Edison Peña**, 34, mine worker
13. **Carlos Barrios**, 27, mine worker
14. **Victor Zamora**, 33, mechanic
15. **Victor Segovia Rojas**, 48, electrician
16. **Daniel Herrera**, 37, driver

17. **Omar Reygadas**, 56 electrician

18. **Esteban Rojas**, 44, maintenance chief

19. **Pablo Rojas**, 45, mine worker

20. **Dario Segovia**, 48, drill operator

21. **Yonni Barrios**, 50, electrician and medical worker

22. **Samuel Ávalos**, 43, mine worker

23. **Carlos Bugueño**, 27, mine worker

24. **José Henríquez**, 54, driller

25. **Renán Ávalos**, 29, mine worker

26. **Claudio Acuña**, 44, mine worker

27. **Franklin Lobos**, 53, driver, former professional soccer player

28. **Richard Villarroel**, 23, mechanic

29. **Juan Aguilar**, 46, supervisor

30. **Raúl Bustos**, 40, hydraulic engineer

31. **Pedro Cortez**, 24, mine worker

32. **Ariel Ticona**, 29, mine worker

33. **Luis Urzúa**, 54, topographer, shift foreman

Finally everything was ready for our departure. A rescue worker explained every step of the process and gave details about what would happen. To get into the cabin of the Phoenix II capsule, we had to put on a helmet with earphones and a wireless microphone, glasses to filter the light outside, a biometric belt, a fireproof thermal suit, and even a support bandage to avoid any thrombosis in the leg muscles. The capsule had a complex communications system and was painted with the colors of the Chilean flag—white, blue, and red.

Having spent sixty-nine days with this group, I knew there were different types of leadership. Some directed the group from a technical perspective, while others were natural leaders. In my case, the Lord gave me the privilege of exercising spiritual leadership within the group. This was so until our very last moment together. Before leaving, I spoke to the group and said, "God has answered our prayer, so no one is leaving this place until we first pray and give thanks to the Lord for blessing this work." Then we spent several minutes praying and asking God for his angels to protect us, and so it happened. Two of the rescue workers who came down to help us also were Christians and joined us in prayer.

*"God has answered our prayer, so no one is leaving this place until we first pray and give thanks to the Lord for blessing this work."*

At last, one by one, we began to leave. After spending so much time together, we began to feel a bit lonely as we watched our coworkers leave. However, we are people who are accustomed to being alone. The important thing was that everything continued to work properly.

At 5:59 p.m. in the afternoon on October 13, 2010, I was the twenty-fourth man to leave the mine. I was lifted to the surface aboard the Phoenix II capsule. I was feeling very happy, at peace, rejoicing in the Lord. The ride took nine minutes, and during the entire journey I glorified God and gave him thanks.

When I arrived at the surface, everyone was yelling at me because I was not saying anything. Most of the men, after their arrival at the surface, had started shouting euphorically. Nevertheless, I arrived calm and happy. The Lord had answered our prayers, and the rescue plan was going according to his design. I give thanks to God for that, and I promise to serve him for the rest of my life.

# CHAPTER 10

## We Come Back
## into the World

After a little more than two months of being trapped at a depth of 2,300 feet underground with thirty-two coworkers, our story had a happy ending. We were successfully removed from the mine. The technicians and rescue workers worked around the clock to achieve this Chilean miracle. At first they had estimated it would take forty-eight hours to lift us out one by one aboard the Phoenix II capsule, but the final rescue operation took less than twenty-four hours.

Chile's national television station broadcast the images of our exit from the tunnel. After we arrived at the surface and stepped out of the capsule, each man was welcomed by his relatives and by dignitaries, including the Minister of Mining, Laurence Golborne, and the president of Chile, Sebastián Piñera. After I saw the president of my country, the ministers, and everyone who took part in our rescue, I was overwhelmed with many emotions. All of these people were part of the team that God used to lift us out of the mine. I am very grateful to all of these men who accomplished all of these things with goodwill and a lot of hard work.

I have been married for many years to Blanca Hettiz, and at the time of the accident we had enjoyed thirty-three years of married life. Seeing her again after everything I had gone through was a very emotional experience. It was a moment full of tenderness and love. Many people consider me to be a very extroverted and loving man, and when I saw my daughters I gave them a big, strong hug. Everyone knows that my heart is full of gratitude.

After getting out of the capsule and greeting those who welcomed us, there was a protocol we had to complete. There were certain security requirements that had to be fulfilled, regardless of our physical condition. Then each of us was placed on a stretcher and taken by ambulance to a nearby hospital, where we spent the next two days getting complete physical examinations. I slept one night at the medical center. The next day, in the afternoon, I returned to the campground to look for my personal belongings, which were still in a locker.

It was very important for me to return there. I was able to meet some of the people and to see the small "city" that had been built around the place. I was also able to get a better idea of how the rescue team had planned the entire operation, witnessing firsthand the fact that the love of people can move mountains and move men to do unprecedented things. It is often true that tragedies such as this cause human beings to unite.

> *The love of people can move mountains and move men to do unprecedented things.*

Later I learned that God also had his people in the campground who were working for him. There were men there who preached the gospel and offered words of encouragement. There were even a lot of people there who gave their lives over to the Lord. God looks for a way of carrying out his purpose — and for that, he needs people who are conscious of the love that he has for them. Out of all the mining accidents that have occurred, this one turned out to be something special. God chose us.

## The Eyes of the World

The national television station of Chile (TVN) estimated that about a billion television viewers were following the rescue story. People from all over the world, including some chiefs of state, had their eyes on this remote part of Chile. From the time the announcement was made that we were still alive, millions of people around the planet followed the details of the rescue operation step-by-step. More than two thousand international reporters from places as far away as China and Turkey arrived at the mine to cover the news. This overwhelmed the media representatives already stationed at the mine who lacked such international credentials. Broadcasts appeared on television monitors in New York, Sydney, London, and Tokyo.

According to press reports, BBC broadcasts often superimposed on the bottom of the screen a scrolling list of headlines about the rescue operation ongoing in Chile, where relatives of the miners and Chilean leaders were awaiting the arrival of the mine workers as if we were national heroes. Something similar happened in Japan, where live reports of the rescue operation were broadcast on television screens. In Australia, reporters for both television and radio stations presented complete coverage of the rescue operation.

Even the president of the United States, Barack Obama, in Washington, D.C., made a statement to the press that he was following the story of the Chilean miners. In a press release published in both

English and Spanish, Obama said, "Our thoughts and prayers are with the brave miners, their family members, and the men and women who have been working so hard to rescue them." Univision, the Spanish language television network in the United States, also presented live broadcasts, along with directions to websites that had more information.

The Venezuelan president Hugo Chávez and the Bolivian president Evo Morales, who was present because one of the miners was Bolivian, also arrived at the site to express their good wishes for the rescue team members and the miners.

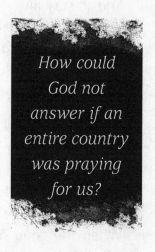

*How could God not answer if an entire country was praying for us?*

However, for me the most important thing was to know that five continents had united in prayer and fasting for us. Hundreds of prayer chain meetings and vigils were held to lift up prayers on our behalf. The whole world — not only the adults, but also the children — witnessed the rescue operation. In every place that I visited after the accident, I learned that the children had been the first to pray for us. How could God not answer if an entire country was praying for us? Certainly our cries heard below the earth were multiplied above the ground.

# God's Eyes
# on my Family

My family was also part of this story. While I was still trapped below, I kept in contact with my daughters and my wife. They informed me of some things that were happening outside. On several occasions, in my letters I gave them instructions about what they should do. I asked them not to get involved in certain things that were not really their business and to stay away from anything that might seem disorderly. I wanted them to stay away from exposing themselves to trouble and to stay calm, participating in the service that was being celebrated above and praising God.

I was worried about the security of my family, but God was watching over them, just as he was watching over me underground. When serious accidents occur inside a mine, all miners know what it means, and we always try to help one another. When my good friends at the El Teniente mine, which is like a second home to me, learned that I was buried in the San José mine, they were stunned. They took up donations to help my family. After I learned of their help, I was very touched.

I also learned that a very good childhood friend, Carlos, whom I had not seen in many years, knew that I was involved in the mining accident at San

José. I did not know it, but he had risen to the rank of colonel of the carabineers, Chile's national police force. Without my knowledge, he took care of my family during the time that I was trapped in the mine. He stationed guards to watch over my daughters continually. This was another sign to me of how God protects his own at all times.

It is always marvelous to see how God works in all things for the good of his children. The human mind cannot understand it, but if we meditate on this promise, we will conclude that everything happens according to the plan of God. I knew the promises that are in the Word of God, which are available to all those who believe and claim his protection for themselves and their families. I had always believed in that promise and was able to validate this truth firsthand after I had returned to the outside world.

As I stop to reflect, I have lived in the same house for many years, and there were no signs of damage after an earthquake shook the city, even though we were near the epicenter of that natural disaster. So how can I not be grateful to God? How can I not believe in his protection? I have believed in this promise, and I always will. On this occasion, I was able to see how God provided a way for my family to get to the campground in Chile's Atacama region, near the city of Caldera. That place was more than 600 miles from Talca, the city where we live, but many people demonstrated their solidarity and came to their aid.

So for me, all of this has been a blessing. Even more important, my wife and my daughters, who were not yet fully committed to involvement in church activities, have drawn much closer to God. Looking back at the day of our final rescue, I can see on videos of the event my wife, Blanca Hettiz, with her arms raised to heaven and giving the glory to God for having taken us out of that place. That was a very positive thing for me. In addition, the Lord has been glorified in the midst of this catastrophe, and many people have come to know him.

## God Made It All Possible

At the time I left the mine, one of the most unforgettable encounters I had was with the president of Chile, who congratulated and hugged me and said, "Thank you, José, because you kept the group united."

I answered, "Give all the thanks to God because he is the one who was with us the entire time."

"Ah! Yes?" he said.

"Yes, certainly that is how it was," I added.

And that is the truth. I am only a vessel for God to use. I am a laborer, a responsible worker, who one day received the Lord and obeyed the Word. From childhood I have seen the miracles and wonders of God. So I did as any Christian would have done. I cried out to God and demonstrated my faith in a positive way. So do not thank me. Give thanks to the Lord. He is the one who took charge of everything down below.

*I am only a vessel for God to use.*

# CHAPTER 11

## An Eyewitness of the Power of God

Anyone might think that after managing to get out of the mine alive the story would be over. Usually that is how a movie ends. Our goal had been achieved, our objective reached, and now we had come to the finale. I thought that after I got out of the hospital I would simply return home, and we would resume the routines of daily life we had before the accident.

Those were my intentions, my expectations, but that is not what happened. I never thought that what we were living through would later be so important and have such a profound impact. But a new story had begun, and I had a role in it. I first became aware of this in Copiapó, where I met with some people whom I never imagined I would encounter.

I never could have imagined that the Lord would use me and send me to other countries and other continents. I am a simple worker who has been given responsibility for the gospel. I am an eyewitness of the power of God. I have tried to be faithful to him, and I believe that God has blessed me, honored me, and answered my prayers. Many people have expressed their incredulity and unbelief, but that does not detract at all from the reality of what happened to us. God worked in our situation. He heard our cries and answered our prayer. That is the most important thing about this story.

I have been ill on several occasions and have been involved in other terrible accidents. Nevertheless, in the midst of all these situations, I have seen the power of God at work. In addition to the things written in his Word, I know in a very personal way that Christ is powerful, so whenever I stop to talk to someone and say, "Christ heals" or "Christ saves," it is because I have experienced this truth in my own life. I am now able to testify to God's power and his love with greater assurance than before, even though God is the one who makes any final decisions regarding people.

> *I never thought that God would call me to fulfill such a glorious purpose:* to be a voice to the nations in the name of Jesus.

In my case, I made a commitment to the Lord and was anointed to give my testimony, but I never imagined I would be used to guide my coworkers to the feet of Christ. I was only a simple accordion player. I never thought that God would call me to fulfill such a glorious purpose: *to be a voice to the nations in the name of Jesus.*

## An Unexpected Anointing

At a meeting with the president of Chile and his ministers, they explained all of the things that had been donated and outlined all of the possibilities and aspects that had been considered when organizing the rescue operation. The project was called "Jonah." We heard the president talking about Jonah, the biblical character. During that meeting I did not say anything. A coworker, Raúl, spoke for me. He expressed our gratitude to all of those present, including the president, who listened attentively and seemed surprised by his statement.

On another afternoon, I met with the chaplain of the Chilean presidential palace, Pastor Alfred Cooper. He introduced himself and asked my opinion about what the president had told us about the rescue operation. I answered that everything seemed good to me, but there was one detail that needed clarification. We needed to "give the honor and the glory to the one who gave the order that the fish should set Jonah free." The people seemed to be praising themselves for everything *they* had done, but the most important thing was missing.

At that meeting something very important happened. Pastor Cooper asked me if I would let him pray for me. Then he asked me, "What would you think, José, if at this moment I anoint you?"

"Pastor, do it. I am the one who would receive the blessings," I answered.

There are no words to describe the moment when he placed his hands on me and declared, "You are a voice to the nations in the name of Jesus."

At that moment I felt the presence of God anointing me. The pastor applauded my faith, telling me that God had opened the door and that many blessings were on the way. Later I understood what he was trying to say. We all believed that we had reached the end of the story, but the truth was that something new had begun in our lives; another stage was upon us.

It is amazing how God mysteriously plans things and has a comprehensive vision of what is going to happen. He tells us that he sees every event before its time, in the middle as it is happening, and also afterward. God plans everything and knows the results ahead of time. He knows what will happen. As the Bible says, God has infinite wisdom, and "the foolishness of God is wiser than human wisdom" (1 Corinthians 1:25). A door was opening, and we needed to take the opportunity to proclaim that if in all these events there is a leading man, a hero, his name is Jesus Christ.

## My Life Has Purpose

I was trained first by my grandfather, later by my parents, and much later by my church setting to serve God. There were leaders who ministered in my life and molded me. While I was inside the mine, I postponed my own interests and placed myself in the hands of God in order to serve my coworkers by using whatever God had placed at my disposal. This was all part of the plan that God had for my life, a plan that began to develop from the time of my birth and was confirmed on the day that I accepted the Lord Jesus Christ into my heart.

When someone accepts Christ, he wants to share with other people what he has felt and experienced. He wants others to experience the same things that God has accomplished in his own life so that they also may have a personal relationship with Jesus. I believe that every person who receives Christ and has that desire in his heart will also possess the certainty, the conviction, that he must share this with others wherever he may be, whether at work, out traveling, or at any other place. This is what happened to me. It is something that was born inside my heart. It comes from an urgent desire to present the living God in such a way that all will receive him. I always have this desire in my heart. The Lord expects us to be instruments in his hands.

While in that dark place, trapped for so many days underground without seeing the light of the sun, I was able to prove to myself that I am willing to witness for the Lord for as long as I am living on this earth. I was also able to put myself in the hands of God and see that this was a very important opportunity, not only for lifting up prayers, but also for preaching the Word and proclaiming the message and purpose of the gospel. We must dare to ask the Lord to allow us to touch the hearts of thousands of people through this message.

I never thought of setting myself up as a prayer leader or a spiritual leader, as the media have described me. I only put myself in the hands of the Lord as a worker, as one who is responsible for the truth. I have never liked taking the lead, and those who know me well know this about me. Nevertheless, in this case the Lord took control of everything, and I only did what was necessary for me to do: leading prayer, talking about the Lord, and preaching his Word. If I am certain of anything, it is that I always emphasized that our God is great and powerful.

Now I have traveled to all the nations, testifying of what I experienced, not because I personally sought the attention, but because this is part of my obedience to God. I have gone out to tell the world about what God did for us. I am a child of God, and I will never deny that. I only did what any child of God would have done, because the Lord has not called us to be cowards, but rather to face these situations as giants and tear down walls in his name.

> *The Lord has not called us to be cowards, but rather to face these situations as giants and tear down walls in his name.*

God prepared me and allowed me to have all these experiences so that I could later give the testimony that I am presenting. God has preserved my life so that I could speak to a generation of leaders within the church, to Christians who are more concerned about having positions of importance and being served by the church than about serving others. Nevertheless, the Word tells us that we should be gentle and humble in heart. That is the secret.

Along with the need to be courageous, we must be imitators of Christ and doers of his Word. Regardless of whether we know much or little about the Bible, we must have love for others, for our neighbors, and also for the gospel and the cause of Christ. We should not be guided by our own interests, which are generally egotistical and can often be stumbling blocks for the work of Christ.

## The Opportunity to Testify

Sometimes people ask me what it feels like to be famous, to have the privilege of being interviewed by the media and to appear on the front page of the newspapers. I have always answered in the same way: "If this fame allows me to testify about Christ, it is welcome, because God has provided it without my having looked for it and without my expecting it. If it is useful that I go anywhere in the world to tell others that Christ lives, reigns, and dwells in the hearts of people, then it is welcome. I see it as an opportunity, a door that God opened, and everything else is included with that."

It is natural for a person who accepts Jesus Christ to tell his friends about his experience. He will tell them, "Listen, Christ has done this in me because he lives and reigns. I did not know him, and today he is working in me. Now I have the firm conviction that he came to my rescue, and I have been able to see with my own eyes that he is a true and living God." When you first experience the love of Christ, your desire often is for others to achieve the same level of understanding that you have attained. And that is a good intention. However, being a Christian also implies being transparent about the love of God toward others. It may mean not keeping what you have received to yourself.

The Bible tells us, "Heal the sick, raise the dead, cleanse those who have leprosy, drive out demons. Freely you have received; freely give" (Matthew 10:8). This is what every Christian must do. We must make known what God is doing, not only for the benefit of our relatives, but also for anyone God has placed in our path.

I do not serve God out of duty but rather out of a heart full of gratitude, not least of all because of the title that he has given us, which we previously lacked, because now we are called "children of God." Recently I have been given titles that I never expected to receive, such as "Illustrious Son" of my city. However, the most beautiful thing in life is to be a child of God. Every person in the world should be able to claim this title and belong to the family of the Lord. This is where each person finds his fulfillment. Without God, we are not worth anything.

Gratitude should always be present in us. Whether we possess many things or lack everything, whether we have difficulties or enjoy smooth sailing, we are always debtors to Christ. God gives us everything that we have in such a way that we can only say he is the provider of all things. All that is required is our willingness. If we serve God in a bad way or with little interest or enthusiasm, the result will be futility. We should always serve God with sincere intentions, with cheerful hearts, and with good attitudes. We should not feel forced or obligated, but our desire should always be to please the invisible God.

While we were still in the depths of the mine, I got together with my coworkers and discussed the unique opportunity we would have to testify to the whole world about what God had done in that place. They were all in agreement with me. This would be our opportunity to speak about Jesus Christ. The Bible tells us that after Jesus healed the sick, they went out testifying and praising God. Immediately after their healing they ran to tell others about what Christ had done for them.

All of those who have had to live through a time of crisis such as this one — a time during which they were rescued, strengthened, and healed by God — should take advantage of these opportunities to give him the honor. In the same way, we must tell the whole world about the role that the Lord played in our story and let others know that he really answered our prayers. Our God is a living God, mighty and powerful, who is always at our side and whose promises are real. We do not need to send him letters or messages. He is there with us at all times. He declares in his Word, "For where two or three gather in my name, there am I with them" (Matthew 18:20).

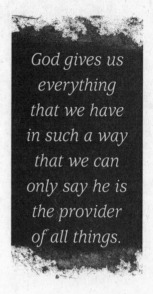

*God gives us everything that we have in such a way that we can only say he is the provider of all things.*

We — the miners who were trapped among solid, impenetrable rocks — called on the name of God, and he was with us. He sent his Spirit, who always accompanies us, no matter where we go.

The first sign that the miners were still alive. This handwritten note will be on display in the Regional Museum of Atacama in Copiapó, Chile.

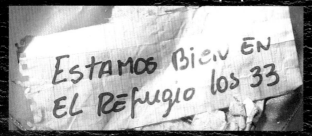

Inside the mine, about 2,300 feet underground, doing special chores.

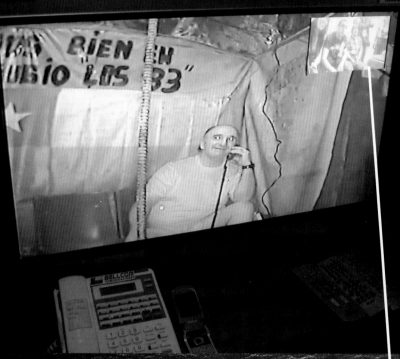

We talked to our families by videoconferencing. It was a very emotional experience to see them all again and to know that they were well.

My granddaughter Catalina waiting for me to leave Camp Hope.

My wife, Blanca Hettiz, holding a Chilean flag that bears my signature along with the signatures of my friends and relatives.

The slogan on the shirt that amazed the world and served to publicly proclaim our thankfulness to God.

"Porque en su mano están las profundidades de la tierra, Y las alturas de los montes son suyas"

De Él, es la Honra y la Gloria

The reverse side of the same shirt displayed the text of Psalm 95:4: "In his hand are the depths of the earth, and the mountain peaks belong to him."

Members of the rescue team working at the mine.

Panoramic view of the San José mine. The tents are part of Camp Hope.

Photographer/Artist: ARIEL MARINKOVIC/Getty Images

The Phoenix 2 capsule that was used during the rescue operation on September 25, 2010.

ARIEL MARINKOVIC/AFP/Getty Images

My first steps after I was successfully lifted out of the mine.

My exit from the Phoenix 2 capsule after being trapped inside the mine for sixty-nine days. President Piñera smiles as he applauds the rescue of Miner No. 24.

A warm greeting from President Piñera after
I left the capsule that brought us to the surface.

Like the rest of the miners, after exiting the mine
I was placed on a stretcher and taken to
a hospital in Copiapó for a physical examination.

The tears of my beautiful granddaughter Catalina and my wife, Blanca Hettiz.

The reunion with my daughters, Hettiz and Karen, after the doctors had finished their medical duties.

With my wife, one of my daughters, and my granddaughter.

During my visit to the mine just days after the rescue.

A friendly hug brought me together with the president of Chile after many days of hope and hard work.

Visiting the Chilean Parliament with the rest of my coworkers who were rescued from the mine.

Presenting my testimony with Pastor Alfred Cooper.

With the deacon of the Durham Cathedral in England.

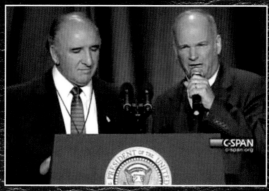

With Pastor Cooper, affirming that GOD ALONE was our refuge, our only resource.

The president of the United States of America, Barack Obama, saying a few words at the National Prayer Breakfast on February 3, 2011.

With Barack Obama, president of the United States, and Pastor Alfred Cooper.

After what happened, we decided to go back to the mine with our families. Together we thanked God.

# CHAPTER 12

## Can Anything Good Come from Talca?

know that I am a sinner who is imperfect before God, but I have always been willing and ready to serve him. Perhaps I am not the most qualified man, but the Lord told me the same thing that he told Moses when Moses complained that he was not eloquent or good with words: "Now go; I will help you speak and will teach you what to say" (Exodus 4:12). I can assure you that this promise has been fulfilled in my life. God has allowed me to travel to many towns and cities, working on many projects in dark and solitary places, in order to mold me to testify to the love and power of God.

While Jesus was preaching here on earth, people questioned who he was and why he was preaching. Some were even saying, "Nazareth! Can anything good come from there?" (John 1:46). Because I am an ordinary man, a miner, people may be asking of me, "Can anything good come from Talca?"

Although the story of my life seemed routine and empty of any major upheavals, everything changed in a matter of seconds. An anointing took place by which I was called to be a voice to the world, taking hope and faith to the members of a group of men who found themselves trapped. I went from being a miner to being an ambassador of Christ to the world.

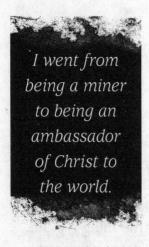

*I went from being a miner to being an ambassador of Christ to the world.*

However, God knows me, and he is aware of my humble heart. He knows that I love him, and it does not matter to me what titles man may bestow. God is sovereign over all of these matters, and many times he pulls us off the church pew to raise us up according to his purpose. So when the pastor suddenly called and said, "We must go to such and such a place to fulfill what God has told me," I answered, "Amen, then we will go. That is what we are here for." And that is how we got started.

The Lord knows how you have served him. He knows your disposition and personality. He knows how you behave at work and how you behave in your personal life. Having seen God at work in my own life on many occasions makes me fully aware that I am a debtor to Christ. I should not be writing these pages, but this was not my plan. It was the plan of God, who loves me and has a purpose for my life. I do not have a lot of advanced learning, nor have I enrolled in a theological studies program, but the Lord chose me and has taken me abroad to many beautiful countries to testify about him and his work.

## My Journeys Begin

One day I received an invitation from Dr. Luis Palau to share my testimony in front of thousands of people at Plaza Italia in the city of Santiago, Chile. The festival leaders also gave me the opportunity to offer a prayer. When I did, the Lord poured out his anointing on the pastors who were behind the platform, as well as on those who were standing at the front. It was a great experience for me to pray for Dr. Palau in the name of the Lord. We all received a great blessing.

There was a moment during the presentation of the testimony when Dr. Palau held the microphone for me while I was talking. I was amazed that someone so well-known and wise, a doctor of the Word, would be so friendly to me and condescend to assist me in that way. He was willing to be an equal to someone like me. He was willing to be a servant so that he could participate in the preaching of the gospel. This man of God has great humility, and this attribute became a part of his silent testimony for thousands of people who were watching him.

After I returned home following this festival, I received an invitation from two young men who wanted to organize a campaign of preaching about Christ. After I observed their enthusiasm and saw how motivated they were about doing something for the Lord, I felt honored. My heart was touched.

Of course I accepted. The only thing I asked was that they cover the cost of travel expenses for my wife and me. On the appointed day we traveled to Antofagasta. The way that everything was organized was like a miracle. A relative of one of the men had donated a room at one of the largest hotels in the city for our lodgings. Another friend paid for our travel fare. In addition to covering the costs of the event, they were also able to give me an offering.

After the event had ended, we celebrated the victory of seeing 366 people surrendering their lives to Christ. Three churches in the area would be responsible for discipleship for these new believers. What we experienced was noteworthy. This was one of the first events to confirm the great challenge that God was placing before me. I believed that the Lord was supporting me, and that was enough for me.

# The Trip to the Holy Land

Through the Israeli embassy in Chile, the government of Israel invited the thirty-three miners and our wives to visit Israel for the purpose of giving thanks to God in that place through our prayers. Unfortunately, only twenty-three of the men who had been trapped inside the mine were able to accept the invitation.

We had received many invitations, but this one was special. It represented a real privilege to be near the place chosen by God and from there to be able to thank all of those who had prayed for us. We wanted to give thanks to God in that chosen place where his Son came to save the world. To be able to visit the places where Jesus walked, preached, and died and was resurrected was a great blessing for us. We saw many sites that are described in the Bible and remembered many of the things that the Word says about those places. I never imagined that one day I would be there. It was a great privilege for all of my coworkers and for me.

We also experienced a water baptism in the Jordan River. There, before being immersed in the waters, we recalled the sixty-nine days that we had spent trapped underground in the Atacama Desert. We felt the presence of the Lord in that place. It was a real joy for me to see many of my coworkers, seventeen in all, along with some of their wives, baptized by immersion in the Jordan River.

During our visit, we met with several important political leaders. When we got off the airplane in Israel, we were greeted by Stas Misezhnikov, who is the Minister of Tourism, and Joaquín Montes, Chilean ambassador to Israel. The people welcomed us with shouts of "Viva Chile" and "Viva Israel." We later visited with the president of Israel, Shimon Peres, as well as with several religious and spiritual leaders. We had to answer many of their questions, and with each answer we praised the King of kings and Lord of lords. We testified about Jesus Christ, who gave his life in that place for all of humanity and was also there with us inside the mine.

> *We testified about Jesus Christ, who gave his life in that place for all of humanity and was also there with us inside the mine.*

God used us as his instrument to unite all of the countries with ties of love and friendship. All of our expenses were covered. There were some people who expressed surprise that an expenditure of this magnitude was made on our behalf. However, the president of Israel said that the expense was minimal and that Israel is a country that unites the world. This was one of the things that I was glad to hear from his lips.

## We Speak to the Hearts of England and Ireland

Through Pastor Alfred Cooper, God ordained a trip to England, because he knows very well what is happening in that country, and he knows the great need there. A nation that formerly sent out Christian missionaries to many countries of the world is currently, because of wars and the changing attitudes of the younger generations, experiencing great indifference toward God. Even the large cathedrals and churches are being used for other purposes and are not fulfilling the purpose for which they were originally built.

Because there is great spiritual coldness there, reaching these people and seeing entire families accept Christ became a big responsibility and a dream of mine. It was also important to go there because both England and Ireland are countries with mining industry traditions. So the people easily identified with us. They were very kind to us, and we felt united by the bonds of working in the same industry.

During the time we were in England, we held

five or six services daily. Holding six meetings in one day was not easy, and physically it was almost unbearable. However, something happened when I took the Bible in my hand and stood in front of the crowds of people. At that instant, I concentrated only on what I had to do. I shared my experience and responded to the restlessness of the hundreds of people who came to learn more about the story of the miners. Everything else became unimportant as God took away any distractions or concerns.

While I was speaking, I felt the flow of God's Spirit. The divine power was at work in me. I could feel it running throughout my body. I was not able to stay silent. I had to take action and testify about the power of God.

We visited the Jesus House, which is a Nigerian congregation, and Saint Paul's Cathedral, where we participated in two meetings, each with three thousand people in attendance. First we prayed for the sick, and then we issued a call for people to give their lives over to Jesus Christ. At that point, hundreds of people came forward to pray at the altar. In every cathedral thousands of people attended our meetings, and many people who were unable to get inside the building watched the testimony on huge screens outside. It was amazing.

Something similar occurred in Ireland. I testified to many people, and on one occasion there were even local miners in the audience. God opened doors and touched hearts. After the meetings, people would come up to greet me and to tell me that it had been thirty-eight years since any religious meetings of that kind had been held there. "This day will be engraved on our minds and hearts," they said. We were impressed by the people's reactions, the love with which they treated us, and the reception that our testimony had there.

The preparations for each event included a lot of prayer. I cried out to the Lord and asked him to use me and to put his Word on my lips. I asked him to give me the strength and power to reach the people in attendance whenever I testified about my life and what God did for me.

I prayed, saying, "Lord, may it not be me, but rather your Spirit, the one who sends the Word and pierces the hearts, independently of the one who is speaking." My desire was that the purpose of the Holy Spirit be fulfilled. I was not interested in whether the attendance was a thousand

> *Our desire was to exalt Christ and to give the glory only to him, because it is easy to fall into the trap of wanting to become the hero.*

or three thousand people. I only wanted to see that the people were ready to accept Jesus. That is something that pierces my heart. My greatest joy and happiness is to see the goal of our preaching fulfilled. At all times throughout that trip our desire was to exalt Christ and to give the glory only to him, because it is easy to fall into the trap of wanting to become the hero.

## An Experience with Obama

As I was preparing to travel to England with Pastor Alfred Cooper, I received a telephone call from the Chilean Minister of Foreign Relations, Alfredo Moreno, who said: "Hello, José! How are you? The president of the United States, Barack Obama, wants you to go and participate in a celebration in Washington D.C. and share your testimony about the things that happened in the San José mine. You have to go. 'Yes' or 'yes?' You must be there."

I explained to him: "I am very sorry, Minister, but it will not be possible. I already have a commitment on that day. I will be traveling to England and Ireland. The tickets have already been issued."

"But José, President Obama specifically asked for you."

"Minister Moreno, if you can resolve this scheduling conflict, I personally would not mind traveling to the United States. Pastor Cooper is the one who coordinated our travel itinerary. I would be willing to travel to the United States with him, but I would not want to go alone. I will give you his telephone number. You can call him and make arrangements with him to resolve this dilemma."

"Say nothing more. I will call Pastor Cooper to see what we can do," the Minister told me.

A few hours later, Pastor Cooper called me and said, "José, one cannot say no to the president. This is a serious matter. This invitation comes with a higher level of urgency."

Later I was told that everything had been arranged. Before traveling to Ireland, we would travel through the city of New York in the United States, and from there we would go to Washington D.C. to participate in the National Prayer Breakfast with President Obama. We boarded the airplane and traveled first-class as if we were two very important celebrities. The pastor laughingly said, "Never in my life have I traveled first-class."

"You see, Pastor? The Lord is treating us too well," I answered.

"How good," he said. "Then we can enjoy it!"

When I got up to give my testimony to the more

than 3,500 people attending the National Prayer Breakfast, I had never been in front of so many people. With so many people sitting in front of you prepared to listen, it is very difficult to pretend that you never get nervous. Prior to my speaking, Pastor Cooper had written an outline to guide my talk. However, I gave it back to him and said, "Thank you, Pastor, but why don't we do the same thing that we have been doing until now? Let the Lord guide us." It was possible that I could get my words all tangled with words that were not mine, so I decided not to read his outline. Pastor Cooper was very understanding about that. So on the morning of the breakfast, in my very simple words I began: "Let us hear the Lord speak, that he may show us what should be said."

My assignment was to tell in a few minutes what happened at the San José mine. I usually told this story in about forty minutes; however, on this day, I was asked to summarize sixty-nine days in only five minutes. The truth is that I took seven minutes because it was impossible for me to tell the story in less time. At the beginning of my speech, I greeted President Obama very respectfully, and I also said good day to his wife. Then I directed my words to the rest of the audience and said, "The story begins like this. It was just a common, ordinary day ..."

I went on to thank them for the support that my

coworkers and I had received from many nations around the world during the long days that we were trapped underground — and especially for NASA's contribution to the design of the capsule that transported us to the surface. I also assured them that God had been with us at all times.

I told them how God had given me the opportunity to pray and to lead my coworkers in prayer, and how this strengthened and prospered us. I told them about how the Lord had touched some people and restored them to good health. Later I described our democratic system for getting agreements approved and making decisions on how to deal with the crisis situation. The audience seemed surprised to hear this, but they liked it very much.

> *"We really only had one alternative, and that was none other than God himself."*

I went on to explain that twenty-two of my coworkers in the mine accepted Christ. I explained how when the capsule was ready to take the first man to the surface, we held one last prayer meeting. Finally, I said, "We really only had one alternative, and that was none other than God himself."

The audience was greatly impressed with the

testimony. I noticed that many among these very important and distinguished people were keenly interested in hearing about our experience. We felt in our hearts that everything had gone very well. The ambassador of Chile to the United States seemed pleased. The president was very warm in his greeting and told me that he was surprised to hear all the things that I was saying. Also attending that event were several presidents of other countries, senators, diplomats, and many other important officials. It was a great blessing to have been there. It was a unique experience.

The interpreter who translated my words into English asked me, "What has been the most surprising thing for you at this meeting?" I answered, "The thing that impresses me most is that a government official loaned us his office for prayer and preparation before the event." This official had provided his office so that we could be calm and spend time in prayer before I presented my testimony in front of all those people. We clearly saw how God had prepared everything so that the audience would be ready to hear what we had to say.

All of those important people also have a lot of spiritual needs. That was one of the reasons that our testimony was so well received. And that is why this message is useful for reaching souls. Through my testimony I want to highlight the person of

Christ and give all the honor and glory to the Lord, because he is the star of everything that has happened in my life and in the San José mine.

## Let the Holy Spirit Have the Microphone

God wants to put his machinery into operation according to his manifold wisdom and deliver it to people who need him. He wants to touch hearts in one way or another. Some people are sad, others anguished and afflicted. Some have no hope and are feeling ill. God wants to speak to all of them. So every time we preach, we must pray and ask him, "Lord, speak," because if we put ourselves in first place, we are only people wanting to impose our own ideas.

> *God wants to put his machinery into operation according to his manifold wisdom and deliver it to people who need him.*

There are times when we may wish to teach something else, but God is telling us, "Without me, you cannot do anything." If we are not in the will of God, even with all the education we may obtain, with everything we can humanly do, we will not get the results God desires. When God uses a person, the message is powerful. The sick will be healed, and the people of God will be blessed as they offer praises to him.

We must not forget that there is a spiritual difference between the Christian and one who is merely a sympathizer of the gospel. God sees the intention of the heart. He sees through any attempt to manipulate or deceive. Whenever someone uses human words instead of trying to reach people by following God's guidance, or seeks to play the leading role in a pulpit, or carries out an activity without the grace of God, he only provokes envy and murmuring from others. True children of God, however, do well in every endeavor. This is something that I have seen and experienced. ✳

So at all times, we must follow the example of Jesus who taught: "The people were amazed at his teaching, because he taught them as one who had authority, not as the teachers of the law" (Mark 1:22). The authority of God was manifest in him. The grace of God is present and active whenever the favor of Christ is on someone, because that person has accepted the beautiful truth that God will use him and allow him to act. God endows such a person with a special understanding and intelligence.

# CHAPTER 13

## Content and Prepared for Whatever the Lord Ordains

Nowadays, whenever there is a crisis, whether economic, technological, or nuclear, many people feel defeated and think that life has ended. However, throughout all of the experiences I have described in these pages, I have learned that when God accepts us as his children, we are his forever. My joy is in knowing that he is our shelter. He is a God who does not lie. We would like to see him, to touch him and embrace him, but that is not yet possible on this side of eternity. Nevertheless, that day will come.

Meanwhile, we must be content with a sense of his presence in our lives and our hearts, and that is what strengthens us. In the midst of crisis, the main thing is not to blame God but rather to try to understand what is happening in the world. The Lord has already ordained the times in which he will do what is written. The Bible is not just paper and ink; it is power and authority. Through its pages I learned that God never abandons us. One way or another, the Lord will make his presence known and will bring blessing out of every situation. He will fulfill his objectives, his purposes, because he has already ordained these things beforehand.

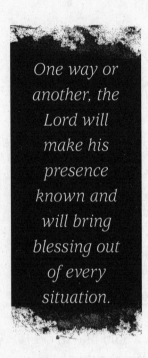

*One way or another, the Lord will make his presence known and will bring blessing out of every situation.*

Each time that we experience conflict, instead of despairing we should remember that the children of God have a purpose in life. We should aspire to put on the mind of Christ — to have a mind that is approved, filled with positive thoughts, in which the Word is constantly flowing. It is important to see that at the moment when these things are happening, God is giving us the solution, because it is he who works in our minds and our attitudes.

When we see Jesus and the people of God who are described in the Scriptures, we learn that a spiritual leader must be loving and respectful and at all times must demonstrate the grace of God. We are only vessels made of clay. Christ is the one who moves in our hearts. We must remain in communion with God so that he will work and complete whatever it is that he wants to do. A man without the support of Christ is nothing. We are only human beings in need of Jesus Christ, the power of God.

That is why I believe that the foundational elements in the formation of a person's character are perseverance, confidence, hope, the Word of God, promises, and faith. We must take hold of the Word that tells us about itself: "Consequently, faith comes from hearing the message, and the message is heard through the word about Christ" (Romans 10:17). The Scriptures also declare, "Your word is a lamp for my feet, a light on my path" (Psalm 119:105). A relationship with the Lord and his Word is what allowed me to overcome in a crisis situation that went on for sixty-nine days, trapped 2,300 feet deep inside of a mountain.

Sometimes we think that we are a certain kind of person, but when we are confronted by difficulties or tests, we change. Suddenly we are full of shouting, anguish, and desperation. We act in a way that reveals to us that we are not who we thought we were. We blame God for what is happening, and it is easy for us to say, "Look how I am trying to be your child!"

That is not the right attitude for a child of God. It is necessary to be faithful all the time and positive about everything. We must wait on the Lord with peace, patience, and confidence that the answer is on the way, because God always has a solution. What is impossible for man is possible for God. We must have a firm and true conviction, a certainty that our God is with us and lives in us. This is what causes us to be different — to have ideas and a different spirit, to speak in another way, to be capable of helping people get out of their negative contexts as we take the light to them.

> *God is pleased with people who place themselves in his hands and put him above all other things in every circumstance of life.*

If we are to serve Christ, we must be willing to set aside the "I." Our egoism must disappear, and we must place ourselves in the hands of the Lord. God is pleased with people who place themselves in his hands and put him above all other things in every aspect and circumstance of life. As we seek the Lord and begin to grow in the things of God, we begin to acquire the three special tools in life that enable us to face any adversities.

*Become persons of prayer.* Prayer for a Christian is as important as the air that he breathes. Prayer oxygenates the spirit; it renews. If I do not go to the fountain, which is Christ himself, how can I communicate with him? How can I be refreshed? How can I be strengthened? How can I stay in shape spiritually? Prayer is the key to opening the door and conversing with God. It is the telephone that keeps me in constant communication with him. While we were trapped inside the mine, I would say to my coworkers, "We must pick up the telephone and communicate with the Lord. We must be certain that God is at work. We will experience his mercy and see that box filled with food." And that is what happened. We all need a word to give us hope and to help us to live lives that are pleasing to God.

*Become persons who treasure the Word of God.* It is necessary to understand and know the Word of God, because it edifies, educates, strengthens, and teaches us how to live and act. The Word is everything. Retaining its contents in our memory helps us in times of crisis, because that is where we will find the secret, the meaning, the significance of what God wants to say. Besides, if we treasure the Word of God in our hearts, we can share it with others.

*Become persons who dare to build churches without buildings.* In the mine, at 2,300 feet underground and surrounded by rocks, we were able to form a church. If we are people of prayer who know the Word and have faith, we can raise up a church wherever we go, regardless of the environment, context, historical era, or any other impediments.

With all of these special elements of preparation in place, I can stand before anyone and say, "Believe in God." I can explain to them who Jesus Christ is. I can assure them from personal experience that he heals. He saved me, freed me and has used me in many ways, among them the desire to give my testimony and preach his Word.

*It was marvelous to serve as a spiritual guide for that group and to edify all of those men with the Word.*

One morning I went to work thinking it would be just another workday, but God had something else prepared for me. A radical change was on the way. Nothing would ever be the same in my life or in the lives of the other men — the thirty-two coworkers who would spend the next sixty-nine days with me trapped underground.

In spite of the difficulties we experienced in the San José mine, I can say that it was marvelous to serve as a spiritual guide for that group and to edify all of those men with the Word, discipling them with love and observing their progress and growth. That was the best thing I could have done during that time. I feel privileged to have devoted myself, as a news reporters said, "to comforting his coworkers with the Word of God."

Many of us are familiar with the parable about the sower who went out to sow seed:

> As he was scattering the seed, some fell along the path, and the birds came and ate it up. Some fell on rocky places, where it did not have much soil. It sprang up quickly, because the soil was shallow. But when the sun came up, the plants were scorched, and they withered because they had no root. Other seed fell among thorns, which grew up and choked the plants. Still other seed fell on good soil, where it produced a crop — a hundred, sixty or thirty times what was sown. Whoever who has ears, let them hear.
>
> MATTHEW 13:4–9

I am only a sower of the good seed. That was my duty inside the mine, and it continues to be my duty outside the mine. Even though my desire is to see the seed grow and immediately bear fruit, I can only repeat what the Word declares: "[I am] confident of this, that he who began a good work in you will carry it on to completion until the day of Christ Jesus" (Philippians 1:6). I believe with all my heart that God will take dominion of those people and in due time will work in them.

As for my future, I do not know what will happen along this road that the Lord has ordained for my life, but I am sure of one thing: If God tells me that I must go back to working in the mines, I will do so. That is my profession. That is where I witnessed God work miracles that I never could have imagined.

# AFTERWORD

## Through the Eyes
## of Blanca Hettiz

The life of José as a miner began before we were married. My brother, who is also a miner, helped him find work at the El Teniente mine. José worked there and also at the El Salvador, El Inca, and El Indio mines, and he also worked in the north. During his many days on the job, he had many accidents, but thanks be to God that everything turned out well.

On this most recent occasion, while at work in the San José mine, my husband already knew that the mine was very dangerous. He had never worked in a mine that was so small and yet in such bad condition. The mine had only one entrance, and there was no other way to get out. The ventilation was very bad, which made the temperature inside extremely high, and the heat was almost unbearable. José had always worked for large mining companies that provided all of the necessary security features and adequate equipment. However, at this job none of those resources were available.

On the day before his work shift was to begin, José would pack and prepare to go to the mine. He traveled first to the city of Santiago; from there he would take a bus to Copiapó. On this occasion, as he prepared to leave, I asked him, "Are you going to take this jacket?"

"No, perhaps on my return trip I will buy another one in Santiago," he answered.

I was worried about him leaving without a coat because it was so cold. "Well," I said, "are you sure that you remembered everything?"

"I have a feeling that I am forgetting something, but it does not matter. I am ready."

José had tried to wait until our daughter Karen came home so that he could say good-bye to her. However, Karen's bus was running later than usual, so he decided that he could not wait any longer and went walking to the bus station. While he was standing there, Karen suddenly arrived, so as it turned out they did have a chance to say good-bye.

That farewell was special, different. He told us later that he felt like something was happening, because everything seemed different. By that time,

José's grandmother had already gone to my mother-in-law's house to warn her that something terrible might happen to my husband and that we should all be very careful. After I heard this, I was very nervous. I would have preferred not to hear that.

After José had gone, he telephoned from Los Vilos and told me, "Now I remember what I forgot." Something like that had never happened before. He had forgotten the most important thing. That was the last time I talked to him before the accident. The following day he entered the mine at eight or nine o'clock in the morning to work.

## The Accident

On the day of the accident I had not turned on the television. I woke up that morning with a lot of pain in my side and almost could not move. I did not hear the news until my nephew called to tell us that an accident had occurred at the mine where José worked. However, there was some confusion. José had told us that the mine was called San Esteban, so at first we thought that the accident was not at the place where he was working.

I turned on the television to see if there was any news. A few minutes later, Karen arrived and told me, "Mother, mother, they just called me to confirm that the accident is definitely at the mine where father is working." My granddaughter Catalina, who was listening, started crying. We decided to turn off the television and began praying together, seated there on the bed. We cried out to God on behalf of all those who were at the site of the accident, humbling ourselves before him and pleading for his protection. Later we decided that it would be necessary to notify our other daughter, Hettiz, who was at her job.

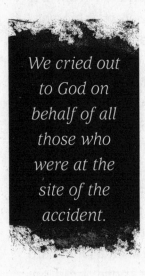

*We cried out to God on behalf of all those who were at the site of the accident.*

A few years earlier, Hettiz had worked in Copiapó, so she knew some people there. After several attempts I was able to reach her, and as calmly as possible I explained, carefully choosing my words so that she would not get too nervous, that there had been an accident at the mine where her father worked. She immediately made contact with some people she knew who confirmed some facts about the accident and that her father was at the mine. They also promised they would keep her informed of everything that was happening there. Then we began to receive telephone calls asking whether my daughters would be traveling to the site of the accident. They wanted to go there, but they had to make arrangements at their respective jobs. As for me, I was not able to go. I could barely move because of the pain in my side. For that reason, my daughters asked me to stay at the house while they went to find out what was happening. Besides, I needed to be at home to take care of my granddaughter, who had to go to school.

The next morning, they were on their way to Copiapó. The Lord had provided the funds for that trip. A brother-in-law and a nephew of José, as well as his brother, were already on their way there. My brother, who is also a miner, also went to offer his help. I placed José in the hands of the Lord and felt a great peace. I am a very sensible person, and I was not feeling any sense of impending doom in my heart, only a little anguish. My prayer was simple: "God, may they not be without air and water." In my heart I knew that José was well, that he was alive.

We continued to pray and started to fast. At church they began to hold prayer vigils for the miners. My daughters called me by telephone and asked me to be careful about watching too much television because they were not presenting clear information about the mine accident. My daughters would keep me properly informed about what was really happening, because the media outlets were too exaggerated, which would only make me too upset if I were to listen to their reports.

I followed my daughters' advice and preferred to wait for their telephone calls. Besides, because I own a business, all of the people who came in would tell me what they had seen on television.

The accident occurred on a Thursday, but until Monday no one in Talca knew that there was a hometown miner among those trapped inside the mine. When the list first appeared on television, they only mentioned the name José without adding his surname or a photograph, even though most of the men appeared on the list with complete names, age, photograph, and place of residence.

On Sunday in the afternoon, Eric, a friend of my daughters, came to ask me how José was, because he had read a few reports listing the miners who were involved in the accident and my husband's name was not on the list. Then I explained that although he might know my husband as Samuel, his first name was José, which is what appeared on the list. Eric told me that he had a friend who worked at the national television station and that if I would authorize him and give him all of the facts, he could call his friend to make sure that the necessary corrections were made to the list. I accepted because it seemed odd that I had not received any notification from the representatives of the mining company.

That same night, at about one o'clock in the morning, some detectives came to my house. I had already gone to bed. My niece, who had come over to stay with me so that I would not be alone, was also in the house. When I went to the door, I encountered a man and a woman who began to ask me some personal questions about José and about the mine and other things about his workplace. They asked why I had not yet traveled to the mine. I explained the reasons, adding that my daughters and several other family members were already there. They asked many questions and then left.

The next day, at nine o'clock in the morning, newspaper reporters began to call. At ten o'clock, I received a phone call from city officials. The mayor of the city and many other people called that morning. Later that afternoon a limousine sent by the city manager arrived to take me to his office, because they wanted to deliver two messages from the government. A niece of mine, who is my social assistant, went along with me, as did a cousin who serves as my business accountant, so the three of us went together.

The city manager wanted to know all of the details because he had been unaware of the situation until then. After that, the rumors flew like a dust storm. The news began to appear on radio and television broadcasts and in the newspapers. The matter did not end there. From that time forward, the whole world seemed to be mobilized, and there would be no more peace and quiet. Reporters from every television channel in the country came to my house. I got telephone calls from Spain and many others places. I do not know how they got my telephone number. I really have no idea.

The city manager offered to assist me. Whenever I might decide it was necessary to travel, I only had to let him know. I told him about my health problems and explained that my daughters were already there. After that, the city manager's office would call me once in a while to tell me that whenever I decided to travel I should let them know because they would provide airplane tickets. My answer was always the same: I will let my daughters make that decision. They would tell me, "Mother, there is nothing to do here. Everything is in the hands of the rescue workers." The only thing we could do was wait.

## The Peace of God on My Life

As the days passed, many people would ask me: "Do you believe that after all this time inside the mine the miners are still alive?" I would answer confidently, "Yes." Then they would look at me with this strange expression on their faces, as if to say, "Poor thing. How nice that she believes that!" Then they would leave.

Even though commentary from around the world was filling my life with concerns, I remembered the words of Pastor Walter, one of the first to arrive after the news became known in Talca. He said to me, "Do not be worried, sister. Only the Lord knows for what purpose he has placed him there. Do not be worried, and we will pray." Pastor Walter anointed me there at my workplace and later went to the house of my mother-in-law to meet with her.

*"Do not be worried, sister. Only the Lord knows for what purpose he has placed him there. Do not be worried, and we will pray."*

After ten days had gone by, a nephew came to tell me that he had dreamed about his uncle and had seen him on a rock. Later, another nephew told me that in a dream he had seen him reading the Bible and talking to several people. Then a niece came and told me that she also had dreamed about him. They all dreamed about José. However, even though he was always present in my dreams, this had never happened to me. A cousin who lives out in the country told me that she had received a word in which it was made known to her that there were two Christians in the mine, and both were well. On that very day there was going to be a prayer meeting and vigil at the church, so we went together. I had asked the Lord to give me dreams and visions, but I had not received anything.

The next day, a Saturday, another prayer vigil was held, and I began to cry out to the Lord, saying: "Lord, why have you given dreams and visions to so many people but have given me nothing? I have always had dreams that were fulfilled." After I said this, I saw José holding his helmet as he left the mine, leaning on his elbows. "Thank you, Lord," I said. That was what I needed to see.

On Sunday afternoon, we received the news that they were all alive and well. I was quietly at my house when the girls called me and said, "Mother, mother, they are all alive and well!"

"How do you know that?" I asked.

"Mother, because we are here. We were among the first to hear the news! Turn on the television," my daughters shouted excitedly.

# Communication and the Waiting

José began to write letters, and the girls would read them to me over the telephone. Then I would dictate to Hettiz the things I wanted to tell him. Then one day I was asked to write a letter in my own handwriting and send it by fax so that they could deliver it to José. I did so, and we also added some photographs.

A few days later, Hettiz told me, "Mother, one of these days I am going to talk to father by telephone. If you want, I will hold up the cell phone so that you can hear him, even though you won't be able to see him."

"Of course! How good! And when will that be?" I said.

On the scheduled day she called me and placed her cell phone near the telephone on which they were communicating, and I could hear him talking as if he were by my side. Such a great feeling! He was so far away in the depths of the mine, and even so I could hear him very well.

Sometime later I was informed that they would soon begin to hold videoconferences. Now I was ready to talk to the city manager to accept his offer of assistance to travel with my granddaughter and my niece to Copiapó.

We arrived at the mine on Friday so that we could be present at the videoconference on Saturday. We were able to arrive before the letters were sent, so I wrote one in which I told him that I would be present the following day at the videoconference, because I did not want him to be overwhelmed by the experience. I also told him that his granddaughter and his niece would be there. In addition, I told him that we had come by airplane. He knows how afraid I am of airplanes, so I imagine that he might have laughed a little.

Our experience the next day was so overwhelming! It was so nice to be able to see him. We all wanted to talk to him. We all wanted to say something. We laughed a lot. After the conference was over, we realized that we had shared a beautiful time together. After we left the videoconference, the psychologist, the doctor, and other personnel were waiting for us. They were monitoring the behavior of the people leaving that place, and they told us we were the happiest group they had seen. We were a visible reflection of the happiness of seeing José again. For me it was very emotional. I was feeling very happy.

As we were leaving, I asked an engineer who

was standing outside, "Excuse me, could you tell me more or less how tall that mountain is there in front of the mine?"

"I estimate about 330 feet," he answered.

"That means that they are seven mountains underground?"

"Yes," the engineer said.

Knowing that made me feel very bad. After all the happiness of seeing my husband again and speaking to him, this awareness of how deep they were underground made me very sad.

## The Last Journey

The next time that we traveled was to bring José home. We lived through a very emotional time when they told us they were ready to bring the miners out. My neighbor, who is a pilot, told me he would take him from the mine to the hospital in Copiapó and that José would be the twenty-fourth man to leave the mine, but that I should not say anything because the official announcement had not yet been made. That was very good news.

On the morning that the miners were to leave the mine, I was feeling very calm and happy. I traveled in a van with my daughters to the camp-ground. Later they took me alone to the place where I would wait, near the site of the drilling that had taken place to reach the miners.

The wife of the president, Cecilia, came to find me. She went with me to the place where the capsule was to arrive and commented that I seemed to be the only person who seemed calm and radiated such peace.

"What are you feeling?" she asked me.

"I am very happy about seeing my husband again," I answered.

"You exude happiness, tranquility, serenity," she said.

"Yes, that is something that only the Lord can give by means of fasting and prayer," I assured her.

And so, walking and conversing, we arrived at the place where the president was standing, and he asked me what José was like. Then I told him that he is a very kind and friendly person and that he likes to be with us at home, that he is such a homebody and has a lot of faith in God. I was busy talking before I realized that all the television cameras were behind me. Then suddenly the president said, "Go over there and look. The capsule is about to arrive."

I approached and saw that the capsule was coming. The men who were working the machine were shouting and looking below, but they were not hearing any answer. At that moment I was flooded with doubts. *Had something happened to him? Perhaps the pressure has gotten to him. I don't know. Why is there no response?* It also seemed to me that it was taking a long time to get him out. I was feeling a little nervous, so I said, "I am not hearing a response!" Then the president talked to someone else standing nearby, who shouted as loudly as possible. It was then that I heard José's response. What great relief I felt! José was on his way up!

My husband's first thought after the door of the capsule opened was to come over and greet me, but he had forgotten that he had to first take off the harness he was wearing. Colonel Baeza, a childhood friend of José, was also there and had obviously wanted to see his old friend leaving the mine, but he could not shout or say anything because the president was there. Then, because there were three or four people from Talca standing near the colonel, he asked them to please shout a greeting with the name of Talca, the miner's place of origin. At first those people did not know what to say, but then suddenly one of them started shouting, "Rah-

rah-rah! Long live the Rangers of Talca!" At that moment José turned around, raised his arm, and greeted them. Perhaps they all thought he was a fan of the Rangers, a popular soccer team. They all laughed a lot. I can only imagine the excitement they might have stirred in Talca when they learned on the television news broadcast that he was a Rangers fan.

José walked forward, and we embraced and gave thanks to God together. All of the people began to shout, "The kiss, the kiss, the kiss!" We kissed and embraced for quite a while. Later, when we read the newspapers, we saw that one of the reporters wrote, "She hugged him and cried for a long time on her husband's shoulder." However, I really did not cry. I was feeling happy.

He whispered in my ear in a way that no camera could overhear and greeted me in the way that he always does: "How are you, *amore mío*?"

I answered, "I have missed you very much. This has been the longest shift that you have ever worked in your life." He laughed a lot at that.

After a while they took him away. About an hour went by, and later we were allowed to greet him in the hospital room that they had prepared for him. Everyone was there at the hospital, all thirty-three miners, as well as all of their families. There were also many reporters and other people.

José was one of the first to be released from the hospital. He did not experience any physical ailments from the accident. The only thing that bothered him a little was the disruption in his patterns of sleep, because after they were able to get electricity inside the mine, they left the lights on all the time, day and night.

## The Return

We traveled to Santiago by airplane, and a large number of news reporters were awaiting our arrival there. We had another big surprise when my cousin called us by telephone to tell us that two vans were coming to take us all back to Talca.

When our airplane landed, the mayor of Maule was waiting for us, along with several people and also one of Jose's sisters. We arrived in Talca by caravan. Along the way some people from the church were waiting to greet us. They followed along in cars and buses. A reception had been organized at the house of my mother-in-law. They closed the whole street, and our relatives were waiting for us, together with many of our neighbors. A few minutes later, we had to leave the party because there was another reception for us at the town plaza. It was a wonderful day.

I never imagined all of the things that we have experienced since then. In my prayers I asked God for the best for José. I prayed that he would be given the ability to testify about everything that he experienced and that he would testify to others about this amazing miracle that God has done for him and his coworkers, as well as celebrate the mercy that God has granted to our family. The Lord is faithful. What we have experienced is truly marvelous. From the time that José left the mine everything has been a great blessing. Not even in my dreams could I have imagined all of these things.

*The Lord
is faithful.
What we have
experienced
is truly
marvelous.*

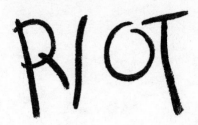

# RIOT

"There's been some talk around of making up patrols to check the estate at night."

"You mean like vigilantes?"

"No, man – *security*." Carlton seemed quite upset that I'd used the term. "Things aren't so bad for you; they leave you guys alone. It's us get hit," he said.

I didn't like this, it sounded too extreme. I said, "That's not the way."

"Tell me what is," he said.

I said, "Well, I don't know. I'm just standing round here fixing your motorbike."

Carlton stared at me with a look I hadn't seen before. He sighed. "You pick your side and then you stick with it."

I looked him in the eye, and felt a chill inside.

"Whose side are you on?" I asked.

# Peter Beere

SCHOLASTIC

Scholastic Children's Books
Scholastic Publications Ltd
7–9 Pratt Street, London NW1 0AE, UK

Scholastic Inc.,
555 Broadway, New York, Ny 100012–3999, USA

Scholastic Canada Ltd,
123 Newkirk Road, Richmond Hill,
Ontario, Canada L4C 3G5

Ashton Scholastic Pty Ltd,
PO Box 579, Gosford, New South Wales,
Australia

Ashton Scholastic Ltd,
Private Bag 92801, Penrose, Auckland,
New Zealand

First published in the UK by Scholastic Publications Ltd, 1994

Copyright © Peter Beere, 1994

ISBN 0 590 54169 2

Phototypeset by Intype, London
Printed in England by Clays Ltd, St Ives plc

10 9 8 7 6 5 4 3 2 1

06336922

# ACKNOWLEDGEMENTS

The quotation on page 95/96 is from the introduction to *Deadly Silence: Black Deaths in Custody* by A. Sivanandan, published in 1991 by the Institute of Race Relations.

*This is for my friend Anne*

# PROLOGUE

On our estate in the evenings the lights which filter out
from the tenement windows are like the worthless jewels
of a cheap paste casket left out in someone's yard. Or
they could be the lights of an ocean liner that has run
aground on a sea of tarmac; or a long-forgotten corpse
that's been disturbed at last by probing searchlights.

They're not the calm eyes of a peaceful building.
They look too harsh for that, too stunned and full of
fright.

Maybe I've got it wrong; they're only rabbit-eyes
gazing out on the wolves.

But at least we don't appear quite so startled now.
Not quite so all-amazed, with our jaws on the floor.

Though lots of things have changed, some things are
still the same. We still keep fighting them . . .

# 1

Old Smoking Joe's café wasn't in any guide that diners-out would buy. Maybe a bug-guide – a bug would like to know where it could go to find the kind of stuff Joe and I served up. That was where I worked, behind the greasy mounds which made up Joe's café.

I'm still employed there, though only in a technical sense since no one's actually laid me off or given me my cards. No one's sorted me out, although the place itself is no longer a café.

Old Smoking Joe hasn't, because he's not around, though I heard two new guys had taken on the lease.

I doubt they'd want it now, looking at the burned-out shell which is all that remains of the café.

It's just a graveyard: a landmark in the street saying that this is where Joe's café used to be.

Joe's not around any more; he's working some place else, serving his lousy food . . .

# 2

Thick heat was pouring down the day someone came in to say Ricky was dead.

"*Ricky?*" I muttered, gawping hard with all the eyes I had, even arching my toes to take a closer look.

I had to check this. "Did you say Ricky's dead?"

"I just said. Ricky's dead."

"I know, but—"

"Ricky's dead. Good God! You deaf or what?"

"No."

"Came right off the roof. Nearly killed someone."

I murmured – "Jesus. Who nearly caught the fall?"

"This big guy walking past. This new guy, Madison."

I muttered, "Madison? I never heard of him."

"No, he's a new geezer who moved into the flats. Came right down past his head and nearly creamed the guy. His blood was everywhere."

"What did he look like?"

"Who? Ricky? Almost dead. They say he said something but no one really heard. His brains were everywhere—"

"Wow!"

"Like a red ice cream."

"Wow!"

"Then old Ricky died."

I could hardly believe it: I'd never heard of death.

Not really right up close, like on our own estate. One day you're walking round, the next you're taking dives from several storeys up.

The guy I was talking to went charging out again, drawn by an ambulance careening past. I wanted to go myself but Smoking Joe said no, we shouldn't interfere.

Which was frustrating, since I was standing there in a deserted place everyone had left.

I thought I'd be the only one who'd never get to see poor Ricky's blood that day . . .

# 3

I saw it later, though, when me and Carlton Strong were ploughing through the heat which builds up through the day and settles on the Grave.

The Grave's the patch of dead land in front of the Schuster block. Not too bad in the day, but quiet as hell at night. At night the creeps come out and hurtle bottles down at anything that moves.

They're really weird guys, and I don't know where they're from. Things were never this bad, just a short while ago. These days, in the Schuster block you really take a chance when you go out at night.

But not on that night, since there were police around, trying to piece together the way that Ricky died. They say he didn't fall, like in some accident. Somebody threw him off.

Somebody hurled him from several storeys up. Which kind of makes you think, like maybe who'll be next? Maybe I'll get thrown off, because that's where I live, high in the Schuster block. It's the worst block on the entire estate, and it was just our luck that's where we were rehoused.

Here comes my mother now, checking that I'm okay. She worries sick for me . . .

"Are you all right?" she asked.

"It's okay, Carlton came. We're all right. Here we are."

I'm a heartache, because I'm all she's got, her only pride and joy. Check the state of me – my ears stick out like flags, I've got some real bad spots – it's the life I lead.

I don't get out enough, that's half the trouble. I don't get any sun. I'm always in old Joe's. He doesn't pay enough that I can take time off, but at least he pays me some.

I'm in that interlude, debating what to do. Should I pack up on school, or try for A levels? I really can't decide.

Carlton keeps telling me that I'd be a fool if I didn't carry on. Carry on to what, though? What's waiting there for me? A world of joy and bliss that's going to save my soul? Somehow I don't think so. I think it's all the same no matter what I do.

He keeps on telling me I'm too cynical but what does Carlton know? He's younger than I am, by a whole fortnight.


My mother grabbed my arm. "Did you see Ricky fall?"

"No."

"Thank goodness for that," she said.

*Thank goodness for what?* I thought, I'd like to have seen him fall. If Ricky was going to die, my watching wouldn't have changed anything. These things are all a part of life's rich tapestry – you have to witness them.

"It was like a nightmare."

"Why, did you see him fall?"

My mother shook her head. "I saw him afterwards." She seemed to be in pain, her face was so crumpled. "I had to have a drink."

My heart went sideways. "What kind of drink?" I asked.

"A cup of tea," she said.

"Thank goodness for that," I sighed. That really shook me; she's a sucker for the booze. And the times she puts us through!

She's spent twelve weeks trying to give it up. Did you hear me then? I said a whole twelve weeks. I know. I've marked them off on the Boots calendar that we keep on the wall.

It's been a nightmare. She gets up in the night and prowls around the place like a tiger in a cage. The first time she did it I thought we'd been bust in, and crawled under the bed.

Carlton said, "Are *you* okay, Mrs Rix? It must have been quite a shock—"

My mother smiled at him. "I'm all right, Carl," she said.

I had to roll my eyes. He really winds me up. He's such a creep sometimes.

"It was just round here . . ." she said, gazing down at the ground like Ricky might be there, still staring up at us. But in fact she had it wrong – it was some distance off. Two policemen marked the spot.

One had some water, and splashed it on the deck like it would be enough to wash the blood away.

It was at about that point that I came to realize I was afraid of blood. I didn't want to see the stuff, not if it looked like blood. Not like the kind of blood that streaks and won't wash off. The second copper stood gazing down at the spot, wiping his foot in it.

"You need a yard brush."

"Where will I get a brush?"

"I've got a brush," said Mum.

"Just leave it, Mum," I said. I took her by the arm and steered her past the spot, still watching anyway. But you couldn't see much, except a dirty stain which in the sodium lights looked like discarded oil.

I'll bet it's out there still, like it will never fade. A birthmark on the earth.

"I'd better shoot off now."

"You're going to watch," I said.

Carlton said – "I might not. I might just go straight home."

"You're going to watch," I said. "Tell me what you find out."

"Yeah, in the mo'," he said.

*In the mo'* – what kind of talk is that? Sometimes he's really weird and just makes these things up.

"Goodnight, Mrs Rix," he said.

"Yes, goodnight Carl," she said. "Just you be careful."

As Carlton left us we clambered up the steps which front the concrete ramp that leads into our block.

We have this wheelchair ramp, but there are six wide steps before you get to it . . .

# 4

I stared down through the lights as policemen tidied up and the crowd disappeared.

It was almost peaceful looking down on the scene, watching the people move like fragments from a dream.

I thought it then and now: this place is like a boat trapped on the ocean.

My mother called out to say my tea was done, and I said, "I just ate something in Smoking Joe's."

She said, "Never mind that, some flesh won't go amiss," and thrust a plate at me.

So I stayed out there, munching on pie and chips while two big mongrel dogs came loping from the gloom. They stalked across the Grave, and one dog cocked its leg on Ricky's patch of blood.

Who was this Ricky?

A black guy of twenty-eight, who I suppose you'd say was quite political.

He tried hard to improve our lives here on the Ridge Estate.

But he's stopped doing that now.

# 5

Early the following day Carlton came with the news that it was murder.

"I already heard that."

"But it's confirmed," he said. "Somebody threw him off from right above your head."

"What do you mean, 'above my head'?"

"Right off of your flat's roof."

"We *are* the roof," I said. "We're on the top floor—"

"So? It was right outside."

"What? Right outside our flat?"

"Yeah, somewhere down this row."

"Wow!"

"It could be your mum."

"Don't be ridiculous."

He's such a jerk sometimes.

"Somebody saw them. Like, three guys struggling."

"Then it can't be my mum."

"And they threw Ricky off. That's why there was no scream, 'cause they knocked Ricky out and then just lobbed him off."

"Wow!" That's a good one. "How do they know they knocked him out?"

"'Cause . . ." Carlton pulled a scowl. "*I don't know that*," he said.

"I thought you knew it all."

"I'm just telling you what I heard. You're such a freak sometimes."

I pulled my clothes on while he was sitting on my bed. Found him sat on my socks. "Get off my socks," I said.

"Has your mum gone to work?"

"This is her morning off. She's gone to Walthamstow."

"What's she gone there for?"

"To see my brother's grave." (He died when I was four; I don't remember him.)

Carlton said, "That's a shame." (I don't know to this day what Carlton meant by that.)

But while I cleaned up I thought about Billy, and how much his death must have affected Mum. She used to see his grave about – what? – twice a year.

She goes more often now.

# 6

Carlton said, "My big mistake was dropping languages to do metalwork."

I muttered, "Uh-huh." (*Blimey, it's so hot today . . .* )

"Because with languages I could have got a job."

"And got the sack in French. It all works out the same."

"See? There you go again. You're such a big down—"

He went to punch my arm, but someone intervened with a blue shopping cart.

Then Carlton hung back to check a music store, and I lurked all alone, staring through veils of heat. Watching the passing cars. Watching the distant sun burning like it was knackered.

The street was hectic, though it was still early. But then it always is in this part of the town. Down here in Camberwell we don't get too much chance to hear the peace and quiet.

Most times you don't notice it, but sometimes all you hear is traffic in your mind.

One day I'll go berserk and never know of it for those car-sounds in my head . . .

# 7

"What are you doing?" he asked.

"Just standing here, thinking."

"That's all you do," he growled. "You'll wear your brain out."

"It's getting friction burns."

Carlton shook with a laugh, and his eyes brightened up. Of all the friends I've had no one lights up the day like Carlton when he laughs.

He stood beside me. We weren't going anywhere. We were just hanging round trying to kill the day. We'd had a vague idea of going to the park, but I got scared of that. Some kid got done there – like he really got done. They stole his jeans and all and tied him to a tree.

You can stuff that for a lark! These are my only jeans – I'm not abandoning them.

Not to mention the indignity. Can you imagine that? Saying: *"I'm over here, and I just got beat up . . . "* And your legs are all bare and all your keks are there for all the world to see.

"What are we going to do?"

(Seventeen times a day I wonder what to do.)

"Do you like poetry?"

Carlton said, "I wrote one once about this neighbourhood."

"Yeah? What was that?" I said.

" 'The last hour of the night'."

"Yeah, really cheerful stuff. I wrote some stuff like that."

"You writing poetry now?"

(I do all kind of things when no one's watching me.)

"Are you writing *poetry*?"

"A little bit," I said.

"I don't like poetry."

So I wasn't going to tell him then, though I really wanted to 'cause I get all screwed up and put it down in words.

Then, *What the heck*! I thought. *I'll tell him anyway.* "I wrote one called 'Poverty'."

Big Carlton nodded, and stared at this old geezer who was searching for some lunch in the waste bins opposite.

"Look at that one there," he said.

"That's what I wrote about."
"You're really weird," he said.

# 8

We sat down on the steps of our old cinema, watching the world go by. I was once out here eating a bag of chips when some great loony guy walked past and clobbered me. I said, "That poem I wrote. Do you want to hear it now?"

"Go on then," Carlton said.

But I forgot things, and got it all mixed up.

I said, "It's written down."

"Saved for posterity."

"It's just for me," I said. (Is that what it's for? To find out who I am?)

I've got a girlfriend, but she's away right now. She's gone to Mablethorpe, which sounds a right old dump. She said it's not too bad on the postcard she sent back. I'm sitting on it now . . .

# 9

When I wandered back home my mum was on her bed, soaking her handkerchief. It still upsets her going to see Billy's grave, and I'm pushed for things I ought to say to her. I try to cheer her up, but underneath it all she needs to be upset. See, my dad dumped us almost six years ago, and I think half the tears are still tied up with that.

I don't know what to do. I don't know what to think about my dad these days.

# 10

I stood silently in Mum's room. The only sign of life was pigeons flying past.

They looked uneasy, as if they felt pursued, though God knows what they thought was up there hunting them. Maybe it's just a game designed to make them feel that they're worth chasing down.

Pigeons and stray dogs, that's the life round here. Long tenements of rooms, with miles of hide and seek.

Hiding away our fears. Searching for little boys who died twelve years ago . . .

## 11

My mother left her bed when someone hit the bell, and life barged in on us.

She ran for the door, plumping her flattened hair, smoothing her crumpled dress. You'd think it was the Pope, but it was just two cops routining Ricky's death.

They had black clipboards on which they jotted notes, and didn't seem to mind that we knew sweet F-all.

She offered them some tea, but they just wandered off.

## 12

I didn't want to leave while Mum was still upset, but in the end I had to go. I was due at Joe's place just after four o'clock, and he would dock my pay if I arrived too late. And she was over it. At least she said she was. She chased me out of the door.

Of course she wasn't, but since I'm just her son sometimes I have to let her act like she's my mum. It's a weird business when you start catching up with where your mother is.

I was really hurtling down our long flight of steps when I almost killed a kid with a bin-bag on his head. He didn't break anything, but he sure screamed a lot.

These kids are everywhere . . .

# 13

That evening at the café a Scotsman came in with a rucksack on his back.

"Have you got some neeps?" he asked.

I stared at him.

"Neeps and tatties," he said.

I kept on looking at him. "If it's not on the board—"

(Some kind of joke that is – there's nothing on the board. In fact there *is* some stuff, but it's just names. Things Joe has picked up and slammed down for effect.

"Artichoke linguini". I don't know what that is. I wouldn't ask for it.)

But this guy stared at me like he was well cheesed off. He said, "Do you do rolls?"

I nodded. "Yes," I said.

"With mashed up spuds and peas?"

"Yes."

"And gravy?" he asked.

"If that's what you want," I shrugged.

And then he boiled up. "Ah, what's the point?" he growled. "It all comes out your bum." (Which kind of makes you think.)

"Don't you want anything?"

"I want some neeps," he snarled. At which point Joe appeared to see what was going on.

"He wants some neeps," I said.

Smoking Joe stared at him. "He wants some what?" he asked.

"Neeps and tatties," I said. "I think it's Scottish food."

Joe didn't seem impressed.

The place had wound down (no wonder, in that heat) and we had quite a crowd of empty chairs watching. They were holding their breath. They live for times like this when violence is abroad.

My boss was panting, which is a dangerous sign and means that Smoking Joe feels he's under threat. He gave a long, deep sigh and glared at the man.

"You should push off," he said.

(That kind of threw him, and almost threw me too.)

"You see that board up there?"

"Yeah," said the Scottish bloke.

"See the 'Artichoke linguini'?"

"Yeah."

Joe snorted a laugh. "We ain't got that either."

Joe's a fairly short guy, but with massive hairy arms, which look like the kind of arms you don't argue with. Joe wouldn't harm a fly, but when you see those arms they're kind of worrying.

He was holding a dishcloth, which he used to wipe his hands, and when he'd finished that he dropped it on the floor. The Scots guy, middle-aged, no more than five foot six, watched it fall all the way.

It was like throwing down a gauntlet, and I could see the Scots guy was considering it.

"Do you want a fight?" he asked.

Joe's lip curled in a sneer. "I wouldn'ta waste my time," he muttered scornfully. He said this in an appalling Italian accent, which is really very weird since Joe was born in Greece. "I justa wiped my hands."

"Well – that's an end to it," the guy said sullenly. But it didn't seem to bother him, because he looked around the place like it was rooms to rent and he was after one. "I'll have a Penguin then. Maybe a mug of tea."

"It's on the house," said Joe.

The Scots guy grunted, giving a grudging nod, and struggled from his pack, which he dropped down by the door. "Do you know some place to stay?"

"You just get booted out?"

"I didn't get back in." The guy looked weary as he ran his hands down his face, seeming much older now than when he first arrived. "I've been away for a while. I just came back again, and the landlord's let my room. He wrapped my stuff up and put it in his shed, which hasn't got a roof, and this is all I've got." He pointed at his pack, which looked kind of forlorn, staring out on the street. "All my belongings—"

"It's very hard," said Joe.

"You can say that again."

But Joe said nothing, he merely poured the tea, and the man stood drinking it, staring at secret things that only he could see. And when he'd finished it he gathered up his pack and shuffled from the place.

I didn't like him, but that's just personal. He might have been okay, and he looked kind of sad.

Smoking Joe gave a sigh as he washed up the mug. "It's getting worse and worse."

I murmured, "What is?"

He muttered, "Everything." Then he picked up his cloth and wandered back to the kitchen.

When he was out there, he shouted through to me. "That guy who died," he said.

I answered, "Ricky."

"Have they got anyone?"

"I don't think so," I said. "They're still out looking."

# 14

On my way home that night I took some lettuce round to this guy Bunny. Bunny's a big bloke who lives three doors away, and shouldn't be round here, though no one kicks him out. We all feel sorry for him, 'cause though he's not too bright, he's a terrific guy.

His mother, Florence, died several years ago, and Bunny lives alone in her two-bedroomed flat. He's keeping rabbits there, of a type called castor rex, which also breaks the rules. Bunny's large kitchen is now a mating ground for thumping castor bucks and gentle castor does. But gentle as they are, nothing could ever be as soft as Bunny is.

"I've brought some leftovers."

"Oh wow, oh great, oh yeah. . ." (He's easily confused.) "Yeah, come in Stevie. I'll put the kettle on." (Bunny's as black as night, and big as mining trucks.) "We'll feed the rabbits now, 'cause they ain't all asleep. I've just been checking them."

I went in sniffing, but couldn't smell anything, which is the major fear that Bunny's neighbours have. (If those things start to smell the Council will descend and Bunny will be out.)

"I've just been cleaning them." (He cleans them every day, and tips the rubbish out on waste ground at the back. One day there'll be a pile so high, low-flying planes will have to swerve round it.)

"Look – put the lettuce down, I'll wash it in the sink." (He washes everything, so the rabbits don't get diseased. As far as rabbits go, Bunny's really good at looking after them. He can tell you everything you'd ever need to know: like how much they should weigh and how to clean their teeth. He'll tell you what you'd need to get the world knee-deep in breeding castor rex.)

"How many have you got now?" I asked, as I put the lettuce down and sat in a chair, facing the breeding pens.

"I've got just seventeen," he said. "Or twenty-two, counting the young ones."

That's not so many. About two years ago the entire Schuster block had rabbits in the rooms. They were out on the stairs, and running down the aisles – rabbits were everywhere.

That piece of waste ground, it was crawling with the things. People came from the press to take pictures of them. But no one ever said who was the cause of it – him and his breeding pens.

But at least he wised up, and came to realize that we're not all as keen on them as he is. Now every second month he stuffs some in a bag and takes them for a ride.

He takes the green bus, which arrows straight through town and stops a minute's walk from Wimble-

don Common. That place is busting now with castor
rex offspring. One day they'll rule the world.

"Do you want some tea?" he asked.

"I'll have a coffee," I said, but this confused him.

So I went for tea, and we sat supping it while worked-
up castor rex did castor rex-type things. They're really
keen on sex. I think if I was God I'd make myself a
buck.

# 15

"This Ricky business," Bunny said seriously, "is a very
bad affair." He looked kind of lonely, that big guy sitting
there, cupping his mug of tea inside his massive hands.
"I don't like things like that. It really worries me. They
might kill off my pets."

"Probably not," I said. "No, I don't think so."

"You don't know though," he said unhappily.

"They won't kill off your pets."

"I hope not," Bunny said. "I can't get to sleep at
nights. I keep on hearing things. I sit up guarding
them."

Bunny looked haunted, as if he faced the fear that

only men with pets can truly contemplate: the fear that all his stock might be killed at one swoop, completely devastated.

I wanted to touch him, but couldn't quite manage it, and just sat at his side, watching his rabbits breed.

There are so many things people can't do. It really baffles me.

# *16*

The next morning, while my poor mum was throwing up like she was about to die, I checked inside her room.

While she bent heaving inside our cramped bathroom, I crawled under her bed and checked her chests of drawers. I was looking for signs and clues that she'd turned to the booze she's tried so hard to quit.

Never thought to find them, because I trust my mum, and after all this time she'd be a fool to drink. But much to my disappointment I found bottles of Scotch drained down to where they stop.

I was so shaken I couldn't move away, and just crouched in her room, unsure of what to do. I didn't feel upset, let down or even mad, just kind of numb.

It was one of those strange instants when things get

turned around, when someone that you like turns round and sneers at you. Some kind of shock sets in, when what you've just unearthed's not what you thought you'd find.

I felt so guilty that she'd slipped back to this, and sensed the pain and shame her heaving signified. She must have felt so low – I know my mother well enough to know that's how she'd feel.

As I glanced upwards, looking towards the door, I knew I couldn't say anything. Having found this out, I'd just have to live with it.

My mum would know I'd found her out. She'd read it in my eyes next time I looked at her. My mother tries so hard and yet it all falls down. Life screws you up sometimes.

# 17

On the Friday afternoon, when my girlfriend Tish came home, I met her in the park.

I was kind of worried with her being away for a week that she'd find someone else or change her mind on me, because when I like a girl a lot I'm always terrified she's going to leave me.

She'll see I'm ordinary, and focus on my spots, and all the little things I try so hard to hide. Like all the secret thoughts that I think no one else has ever thought about. I feel the whole world is hunting after her, trying to tempt her off and cast me in the shade. They'll make me look too dull, and they'll have perfect skin. She'll see how scared I am.

The whole world scares me, plus all that walks on it. War is terrifying, and we don't have one now. I'm scared a war will start and I'll be called up and die from poisoned gas.

I might go crazy and go and *find* a war, because I'll get so caught up with taking someone's side. Though I dream fierce and tough and heroes are my friends, beneath it I'm scared. I jot down poetry to try to compensate, writing about doom and death and other cheerful things. (I'm not a gloomy guy, but I think deep inside I'm quite serious.)

So I looked in a mirror for maybe sixteen hours, picking out all the things which might turn Tish away. And for the next ten hours I tried to put them right, hoping for miracles.

My hair's a problem as it kind of waves a bit, and I spend half my life trying to make it straight. I stick it down with Sellotape like I'm wrapping up my head to post it off. And my skin's dicey and I don't trust it much, and think each time I wake up I'll have a few more spots.

(My mother says they're fine, but then it's not her face they're bothering.)

As for the rest of me, it's fairly ordinary. I'm about five foot eight with light brown hair. My eyes are keen and grey (my mother says they're blue) and my nose is slightly bent.

When I'd finally exhausted the worst of the possibilities, and smoothed down all I could and squeezed out all I dared, I pulled a jacket on because it looked like rain, and ran down to the park. I kind of jogged down because that looks more cool; it's only kids who run, and vandals clearing off. In fact it's more a walk that I've developed myself. A really speedy walk.

Tish wasn't down there, but then she wouldn't be – I'm always early. That didn't stop me from chewing off my nails because I thought I'd been dumped. I think that every time. It always amazes me when Tish comes walking up, beaming her stunning smile.

I watched an old man trying to feed the ducks while some kid's crazy dog ran round attacking them. The promised rain cried off and air reached furnace-heat beneath a blazing sky.

But I kept watching, pretending not to watch, while staring really hard the way that Tish would come. And I paced on the spot, pretending not to pace, all knotted up inside.

# 18

Tish is approaching now, she's heading right for me. It's the big moment.

She's going to dump me or – what's she going to do? It's only been a week but it seems like seven years. She's wearing pale pink shorts and a really tight white top. She's had her hair streaked blonde . . .

I feel so helpless, and blurt out, "How've you been?"

"Yes, I'm okay," she says.

(That isn't what I asked.)

"I really missed you, Tish."

"I missed you, too," she says.

"I *really* missed you."

"I brought you a present."

"A stick of rock," I say. (Well, that's a change, isn't it? A stick of seaside rock. Don't go too mad, will you? Don't spend some dosh on me.)

"Something's inside it. We went to this rock place, and I asked the man if he could hide a gift inside a stick of rock."

"What's it got?" I say.

"You'll have to wait and see. It's a surprise," she says.

I try to snatch it, but she twists in the sun and I see all the shape of her body through her top.

After a week apart I grab for her instead and, *Stuff the rock!* I think.

## 19

*On 25 April 1989, Italian MP and former porno star Ilona Staller released a white dove to mark the departure of Soviet troops from Hungary. It sat in the road and was crushed by the leading tank.*

I put my library book down.

*I know what you mean*, I thought. *I've had some days like that.*

But happily this day wasn't one of them, because my girl came back and kissed me like a dream. And she brought seaside rock specially made for me, with a gift locked inside.

It was a tiny gold heart, a gleaming locket heart. The kind of little heart which says, "This heart's for you." And I thought – blooming heck! I wish I'd thought of that before she thought of it.

I was so knocked out I had to phone her up, even though it wasn't long since we'd dragged out "goodbye". She was right by the phone, as if she knew I'd call.

"I found the heart," I said.

Tish sounded happy. "It's solid gold," she said.

(*Gosh! Better than I thought.*) "Yes, I know that," I said.

"Did you get me something?"

"Well – no. I thought of it, but then I wasn't sure."

(I could hear music . . . )

"What weren't you sure about?"

"I just – I just got scared." (Why does that sound so limp?) "I thought, while you're away with all those other guys . . . Daft kinds of things like that."

"Why don't you trust me?" (The music came again. Tish had some music on, and it came down the phone. I had no music on because my set packed up when I fell over it.)

I said, "I trust you. It's all those other guys."

"Why do you think like that?"

(*Why is this going wrong?*)

"It's just while you're away."

(My heart sank to my boots. I really hate this stuff.)

We shared a silence.

"Are you still there?" I asked.

"Yes, I'm still here," she said, but in a brittle way, because she'd only just come home and we'd walked up to the brink of a stupid argument. "It's you I go with."

"I'll get you something now."

"It doesn't matter now. I just thought that you might."

"Well, yes, I wanted to. It's just I didn't know—"

"Know what?"

"What I should get."

Another long pause came while I stared at our hall wall, and the music in her room deepened and then packed up. I could hear breathing sounds as if she was waiting for me to say something.

"I really missed you," she whispered finally.

"I missed you, too," I said.

"That's why I bought the heart."

"I could buy you one too—"

"Don't buy me anything. It doesn't matter now."

All of this changing and chopping bothers me. It's hard enough for me to follow where *I* am. When Tish starts changing too I lapse into a state near to depression.

"Are we still talking?"

"I've not hung up," she said.

"Shall we go out tomorrow? Where would you like to go?"

"I need to buy a dress."

Oh, hell! It would be that.

"Okay," I mumbled back.

# 20

My half-argument with Tish kept dragging on and on, like it would never leave.

Somewhere in Brixton it lapsed into a mood and we

trudged around the shops as though we'd barely met. Tish couldn't find her dress, and the heat was sapping me so that I lost interest.

We were just strangers trailing from store to store, growling out stilted words when we were forced to talk, and I wished she'd walk away, proving all my fears that she wanted someone new.

I don't enjoy them, these rootless, jealous moods which I whip from my hat like squirming green rabbits. But they're there all the time, like I just can't relax.

(*Why not? Because I'm afraid.*)

In an attempt to cheer us up I offered Tish a Coke at the next place we passed. Two long-haired Asian boys seemed to have claimed the floor, and were causing trouble by simply standing there. (I've seen all this before, working at Smoking Joe's – people looking for fights.)

"Why don't you want to sit down?" Tish asked as I hung back.

"We should stay by the door."

"My feet are killing me."

So I sat down reluctantly by the ledge which runs around the walls.

I kept looking over to where the Asian boys were being far too loud, and splashing Coke around. I thought they'd lost their minds, because there were four skinheads sitting in a back booth. The yobs were staring with that despising look which says, *I'll only stop when*

*I've hurt everyone. I don't like anyone at all, not even my
own friends. Not even myself much.*

A part of me wanted to say, "You two are asking for
it," and part wanted to watch.

But the air of tension made this impossible. I said,
"Let's find your dress—"

"I'm too tired," Tish said. "I saw two that I like. I'll
come back another time and have a look at them."

"Why don't we go then if you're feeling so tired?"

"I haven't finished this." (Tish showed her half-drunk
Coke.)

"There's going to be a fight."

"Where?" Tish turned.

"Those two guys there," I said. They were like two
pigeons strutting in front of cats, too confident by half,
too smug with what they had – which was two pigeon
brains cursed with the idea that they were eagles.

I could map the whole thing, it's so inevitable. Sure
enough, a guy rose up and left the booth. He didn't say
too much. His three friends stared at him. Everyone
else looked on.

The tall guy sauntered across the black-tiled floor,
his thumbs hooked in his jeans, his canvas coat shoved
back. The lights behind his back shone on his stubbled
bonce, turning it silver.

As he walked slowly towards the Asian youths his
boots reflected light like they were black mirrors. He
must have spent half his life getting a sheen like that,
cleaning his combat boots . . .

Tish grabbed my shoulder. "We should get out of here."

"Too late," I murmured.

The really strange thing was that the Asian guys seemed quite oblivious to what was going on. They occupied the floor like two smooth rich geezers, safe behind bodyguards. They were really laughing, swinging black leather coats; their eyes were gleaming coals inside their bright faces.

I thought, *Those fine features are going to turn to pulp when that guy head-butts them.*

Which is what he planned to do; you could see it in his eyes. He was going to walk up there and simply head-butt them. He was going to bust noses, and when they doubled up he and his mates would lay into them.

It was so simple and so predictable. I must have seen that move a dozen times before. But at the last instant one of the Asian youths turned round, there was a flash of steel, and his half-finished Coke was flung across the room. He kicked a table back, spilling a plate of chips and beans into someone's lap and swung his leather coat like a toreador's cloak.

"*Come on then, white boy!*" he started screaming. "*Come on, come on, come on! Let's get it over with!*"

A silence deeper than a tomb descended on the place. No one moved. The shaking, thin guy stood showing all his teeth in a triumphant grin. He kept on waving the knife before the yob, and kicked another plate into someone's lap. Then the two guys ran out and the four skinheads roared and took off after them.

The fight had passed by like a swift summer shower, and everyone inside began to laugh and shake. I took Tish by the arm and pulled her from her seat.

"Let's just go home," I said.

# 21

I was still thinking about the fight as I stood in Joe's doorway while he worked out the cash. It was near to closing, and the place was still as death. The street lamps from outside cast an unwholesome glow. Joe sang some dirge-like song he'd made up himself for the occasion.

I stared upwards, beyond the roofs and lights, watching the coal-black sky lurking beyond the glow. Tish would be out with friends; Carlton was going out to some all-night party.

I turned to watch Joe. "Don't you get scared?" I said. "Walking the streets at night with all that cash on you?"

He left some in the till in case the place got robbed.

"Who's going to bother me?"

I shrugged my shoulders. "There's muggings all the time."

Joe tucked his cash away. "Nobody bothers me." His dark eyes glanced my way. "I've always got my stick."

"What stick is that?" I asked.

Joe started laughing, and tapped his trouser-fronts. "I've got a stick in here to frighten muggers off!"

Not too much of a joke, but it made Joe happy. He switched the main lights off.

Then he stood by me watching the Ridge Estate, like some lit-up disgrace across the street. The only sign of life was speeding taxi-cabs, and drunks heading for home.

"What are you thinking?"

(About my girlfriend, Tish. How much a car will cost. All of the usual things.)

Joe took me by surprise by giving me five pounds.

"What's this for, Joe?" I asked.

"For all your honesty." He tapped me on the cheek. "Good boys are hard to find. I don't pay you enough."

Then he was locking up while I wandered away, wondering what had brought that on.

# 22

Early next morning, while I was still in bed, I heard a crashing sound. I thought my mother was banging round again, looking for pills or booze or some way to her feet, but when the sound resumed it came from well away, along our landing.

I checked the daylight, but the clock said six-seventeen on Sunday morning. No time to be awake, called from exotic dreams, so I slid back again.

# 23

"You heard the latest news?"

I squinted blearily. "What news?" I murmured.

I was in my underpants. It was barely nine, and the sun was glowering down like it detested me. My hair was in a mess, bad tastes were in my mouth, fog banks were in my mind.

I'm an accident at that hour of the day, but Carlton's so alert it almost makes you sick. He was dancing up and down. I stepped into his shade. "What are you doing here?"

"You haven't heard, then?"

"Of course I haven't heard. I just said—" (once again I squinted at the sun) "do you know what time this is? This is my Sunday off. What's this I haven't heard?"

Carlton kept dancing, like he'd lost his mind, and his excited air was getting on my nerves. He said, "Can I come in?"

"Well, sure, why not?" I said, being sarcastic.

But that was wasted, because he just walked in as if he owned the place and I was his guest.

"I'll put the kettle on."

"Why not? Feel right at home. Why don't you make some toast?"

I slumped down wearily in a straight hard-backed chair, and put some music on to jerk myself awake. But all I got was crones singing about the blues in way down New Orleans.

"You haven't heard then?"

"I just said!" (Honestly, he was really pushing me, driving me up the wall.)

But he'd stopped dancing now. He wasn't making toast. He said, "That fuss today."

I said, "I heard it. The crashing round and things."

"The police picked Bunny up. They've got him in the cells. They say he killed Ricky. They dragged him out of bed, wrapped in a blanket."

My mother came in then. "Oh, hello, Carl," she said.

"They've just picked Bunny up for Ricky's death," I said.

"Who's just picked Bunny up?"

"The police."

"That can't be right. He's not a murderer."

"Yeah, that's what I thought, but they've got him down the nick."

"They've got who down the nick?"

"Bunny!" I said again.

"There must be some mistake." My mother looked bemused. She often does, really.

She pulled a chair out and sat down opposite, her thick blue dressing-gown bunched up around her chest. Her hair looked worse than mine, and mine was pretty bad.

"Have you made tea?" she asked.

"Carlton's just made it."

"I made coffee," he said.

"Well, make tea for my mum!"

"Oh, okay," he replied.

"Where did you hear all this?"

"I heard it," Carlton said. "It's all round the estate. People were really stunned."

"No wonder," Mum replied. "It doesn't make much sense. What did they pick Bunny for?"

"Because he's docile," I muttered gloomily.

"Is this the tea in here?"

"No, that's the bran," I said. "What kind of tea do you use?"

"I just thought – never mind." Carlton lapsed into silence.

So we all sat there, perusing our own thoughts, which in my case at least revolved around castor rex.

"What will they do with them?"

"With what?"

"With Bunny's pets."

"Who knows?" Carlton replied.

# 24

Later that afternoon, not knowing what to do, I went to Smoking Joe's. I had phoned Tish and arranged to meet her there. We could have "Joe's Special" (just £1.99). We could drink lukewarm Coke from the free-zer-from-the-Ark which often doesn't work.

Joe's wife was in there, which was a major scare, because she's a strange woman who frightens me and Joe. Two or three times a month she comes to check to see if he's been fiddling her.

"*Ah, my bambino!*" she said when she saw me. (All this Italian stuff was really puzzling me.) "How are you doing, sweet?"

"I'm doing fine," I said.

"Good, good, you pretty boy." As I took a back chair to keep out of the way (Sundays are really quiet; sometimes just Joe's in here) Mrs Joe followed me. "This Joe – this man of mine – has he been cheating me?"

"No, I don't think so . . ." (Joe guffawed heartily.)

"He's a bad kind of man. The worst kind of a man. Does he pay you enough?" (She always asks me this, but more money never comes.) She primped her wild hair (which is a shocking shade of gold) and heaved her bosom straight (which seems hard to control) then straightened up the chairs, which looked okay to me, and kicked the freezer door.

She let out a low moan. "What a big dump," she groaned. "No wonder no one comes. This is a tragedy." As she tried the freezer door it came loose in her hand. "What is this place?" she sighed.

I checked the wristwatch my dad sent me, and it said after one. Tish would be a while yet, trying to dodge the Sunday lunch which her mum seems to think is a necessity. I had about an hour to watch Joe and his wife, and wonder how they were.

*Are those two happy?* (They seem to row a lot.) *Could they survive alone?* (Somehow I don't think so.) *Why have they got no kids?* (Why did I get this watch? Just my dad's guilt, perhaps.)

I sat and checked it, wondering how cheap it was, because my absent dad's not a generous man. It was a Lorus Quartz, which looked okay to me, but then you never know. He probably bought it from some guy at the track. My dad loves the dogs more than he ever loved his son. We had a dog ourselves which he tried hard to train, but it just messed everywhere.

I don't think I like him. In fact, I'm sure I don't. But I'm still curious about the life he leads. He's never remarried and, from what I can tell, he doesn't know anyone.

He lives in a hostel and hasn't got a job, and sometimes I'm confused by simply being his son. We've got no common ground – nothing which would point out that we're related.

I don't think I miss him but I'm unsure for Mum, because I still believe she hopes he'll come back. I can't think why this is, except his lousy love's better than loneliness.

Somebody comes in, but it's not my girlfriend Tish, it's some other girl.

I pulled my chair in as close as I could get, and hugged the table. This Bunny business – could this be possible? Could Bunny really be a killer in our midst? Could he have grabbed Ricky and thrown him off the edge for simply – doing what? Abusing rabbits and making a run at them, kicking a little one?

I couldn't see it, though I could picture it – by which I mean to say I couldn't believe it. I could watch the act occur in pictures in my mind, but not inside my heart. Bunny's so gentle, he wouldn't harm a fly. But maybe – what goes on in people's darkest hearts? What trigger could be pulled to unleash killing rage? Could I kill to survive?

I pulled some mints out and sucked them, afraid that Tish would smell the garlic on my breath. I'd had some garlic bread just before I came out. It was all I could find.

"This Bunny business—"

I glanced across the room. That was what Bunny had said, except he'd said "Ricky".

Joe said, "They picked him up?"

I said, "Yes, so I heard."

Joe said, "Do you see that?"

I didn't answer because then Tish arrived, and Mrs Joe marched up and said, "What do you want?"

Tish said, "I'm meeting *him*."

"Oh, my bambino boy. He's such a charm," she said.

# 25

On the Monday morning (blood-hot day, clear blue sky) was Ricky's funeral.

"Are you going to go, Mum?"

"I didn't know the boy. I don't like funerals."

"He wasn't a boy, Mum; the guy was twenty-eight."

"Twenty-eight, thirty-six, what does it matter?" she said.

"I thought I might go down."

"What for?"

"I've never been . . ." I let it drop at that. I'd been to a funeral when I was only four, watching my kid brother slide to his fiery pit. I don't remember much, but when I picture it I see red flames rise.

"I kind of knew him. I've seen the guy around."

"Funerals are sad affairs."

"I guess," I mumbled back.

"Is Carlton going too?"

"Yes, he'll be at the front. There's a procession."

My mother looked up. "What will you wear?" she asked.

"I thought I'd go like this." (White T-shirt, pale blue jeans.)

"You washed behind your ears?"

I grinned. "Behind my ears."

"Don't be back late," she said.

Then when I went out I felt a bit confused. Was I supposed to watch, or stay there with my mum? Was that a strange moment that she and I just shared?

Kind of got lost somewhere . . .

"Cheer up, misery!" someone said cheerfully. "It might never happen."

I gave a half-smile, because I wasn't really sad, but something in the air just kind of got to me. Maybe the thought of death makes you think about change, and what change might bring.

Things do look different when little changes come, and things change all the time, while we strive to catch up. Not with great crashing roars, but little tiny sounds, like half-heard whispers.

From tiny spark plugs do mighty engines run, and sometimes just a spark starts off a forest fire. Being so close to death made me ponder a while about all things mortal.

But my thoughts soon came back as I stood in the Grave amongst the mourners. I wasn't actually a formal part of this, and only tagged along from curiosity. This kind of happening draws people from the flats like vultures.

We all come to latch on to other people's grief, like it's a carnival thrown for our benefit. We stare at others' pain while feeling none ourselves, because we're immune to it. We're just glad it wasn't us. Glad that this time at least they're not staring at us.

I spotted Carl somewhere towards the back of the crowd, wearing his formal jeans.

The hearse was interesting. It's an eerie thing – a silent car of death, which trundles round the world picking up on odd things.

It seems a smart car. A thoughtful kind of car. A car with peace inside, which I guess corpses like. Who'd want to be a corpse packed on the number 19 bus with hordes of passengers?

I remember once hearing that hearses have a space for carrying a corpse concealed from normal view. Sometimes you see a hearse with no coffin on board, but there's a stiff in it. It's in a long trunk hidden beneath the floor. Maybe someone's in there who's had an autopsy. They're bundled up in cloth or in a body bag, on their way home again.

A million bouquets were heaped inside the hearse, like Ricky's better known than – I don't know. Bigger than royal princes or some great head of state. Bigger than war heroes.

And in the graveyard there's – what? Two hundred heads? Four hundred gawking eyes clocking the crowded space. No press reporters. Though it's big to us, it's pretty small news, I guess.

(*"Did you know Ricky well?"*

*"Yes, we were close,"* I said, *though this was quite a lie . . .* )

# 26

The heat which came with dawn thickened throughout the day, and we made quite a crowd. There were old ladies bent over walking sticks; hordes of kids running round like they were chasing things; tall black guys looking cool in washed-out Levi jeans and Reebok training boots.

I saw some old men dressed up in charcoal suits, gazing towards the sun, wondering when they would melt.

I saw a man with chains like he's our local mayor, stripped to his shirt sleeves.

Then, as we moved off, I heard a cry ring out. Somebody on a roof was yelling down on us. The hearse kept moving, but those towards the rear were staring upwards.

I didn't catch it, the first time he yelled, but then he called again while all the people watched. Shouting the kind of things that I thought should have died when the Third Reich tumbled.

Why did he do this thing at someone's funeral? Why did he feel the need to mock at someone's grief?

The shocked thought dawned on me that it was worse than that. This guy was gloating.

He was some racist who'd come out specially to heap abuse and scorn on those walking below. He'd picked them out for hate because their skins were black, and he's a white guy.

And as I looked around me, people just carried on, while I felt sick inside with anger and dismay. Those people were my friends, they were not black or white. They were my neighbours.

So I glared upwards, trying to breathe my hate, but I heard somebody say, "Leave it, just carry on."

# 27

Next day I sat at a table in Smoking Joe's. I still felt quite upset.

Joe wandered over because the place was quiet, and he was feeling bored and looking for a chat.

"How did it go?" he asked.

"Just someone's funeral. It went okay, I guess," I said, breaking up a pretzel.

But Joe saw through me. He wiped away the pretzel crumbs and leaned in to ask, "Don't you like funerals?"

What could I say to him? There are so many things it's hard to list them all . . .

*I don't like morons who stand up on the roof: skinheads with thick black boots and guys who carry knives. I don't like walnut whips or wondering whether Tish will find somebody new.*

*I don't like bear-baiting, bull-fighting, snotty kids or using dirty lifts. I don't like coming home to find someone else has scoffed all my porridge.*

*I do like dreaming and looking at girls' legs, and wishing I was king so I could change the world. I'd wipe out all the crime and outlaw all the hate and breed blue whales again.*

*I'd erect houses which gave you room to move; transform the Ridge Estate into a grassy park. I'd have the greatest minds this world has ever known find cures for acne.*

*But most of all, though, I'd move far away – somewhere with sand and sea and blue skies overhead.*

*And girls with long slim legs, and me so tanned and fit I'd make a surfer sick . . .*

I slowly raised my gaze until it reached the furze of Joe's thick chin-stubble. He's a good guy, although he keeps me poor and never pays enough for all the hours I do. Perhaps, without my dad, I need a man like Joe to fill me in on things. He's not a smart man, but he's a decent bloke who knows what's right and wrong and tries to do his best.

I said, "I want to know why people seem so keen on finding things to hate."

"You mean like people?" (Joe watched me carefully.)

"Yes, people and their skins, their homes, the clothes they wear. Why can't we just get on? Why do we have to fight and screw up everything?"

(The half-glass door swung back as two young Asian kids came in looking for change.)

Joe tugged his trousers. "You really want to know?"

"Yes." (Maybe Joe *does* know; he looks like he might know.)

"This is a tricky one. I'll have to think on it."

"I need to know right now."

There was a long pause while Joe strained for the words to help explain something so inexplicable. Then, looking in my eyes, he said, "Don't think of this. It cannot be explained."

Another long pause. (*What kind of answer's that?*) "Is that the best you've got?"

"What do you want?" he asked. "I run a café here, not sit at God's right hand. Ask Him yourself, Stevie."

Then Joe went striding away to serve someone, knowing he'd failed to answer me. But he was right, really; you'd have to be a god to know answers like that.

# 28

On my way home that night I met two hairless guys who didn't smile too much. I was walking through the Grave, beneath the overhang formed by the Schuster block. (The ground floor has a strip matching the aisles above, flanked by concrete pillars.)

The lights here hardly ever work – they've been smashed so much they just gave up the ghost. Instead of a safe passage there's a long gauntlet of gloom to cross. The Council's abandoned attempts to beat the gloom – hard as they try the yobs try harder still, and on bright summer days the very air suggests dark nights and doom.

I know at one time, before we moved in here, some jerk threw cats and dogs from the roof above. They used to crash down here and got kicked in the shade so no one stepped on them.

The place became a graveyard for people's cats and dogs, and the jerk who did it now runs a hardware store.

So I don't linger when it gets dark outside, I just scurry through the gloom towards the swinging doors. But if I hear a sound, I can't help glancing up in case a poodle comes hurtling down.

Somebody called me – or maybe someone else, because when I looked round I saw no one I knew. But as I hurried on I slammed into the chest of the first hairless guy.

He had a lead chest, or something just as hard, because I nearly smashed my ribs when I crashed into him. He didn't look amused. I said, "Oh, sorry, mate."

"You must be Stevie Rix."

This made me thoughtful. I said, "Yes – possibly."

He said, "We thought you were," and pushed me in the chest.

I didn't need that stuff, and if I'd been tougher I would have clobbered them.

But since I wasn't, I simply stared at them, checking

their black blousons and manly studded belts. They both had hair so short you'd need a microscope to track down where it lay. They looked like jerks to me.

But they were big jerks – fat, tough and mean. The kind of fearsome jerks that scare small guys like me. I got that sick feeling that, when you've had it once, you hope will stay away.

This was a showdown outside the Schuster block, and I wouldn't waste any cash through betting on my side. You didn't need Einstein to say what was coming next. Those guys weren't Jesus-freaks.

"What do you want?" I said.

"What do you think?" one snarled. "We want to talk to you."

Of course at that point I should have ducked and run, and spent the next ten days hiding inside my room; but one guy had my arm and steered me towards a darker gloom.

In someone's doorway these men gave me a warning. They said, "People round here, who don't like nigs and chinks, like nigger-lovers even less. They don't like white guys sucking up to the blacks. They don't like *our* people mixing with their people. They don't like wogs and chinks trying to take over a land that's English."

"But Carlton's English—" I tried to stammer out.

"England's a *white* nation. You don't get English blacks. What you get's nigger boys pretending to *be* white, who laugh behind our backs. They get the best treatment 'cause you feel sorry for them, and they take up half the jobs that should go to our own. They're here to start a war, and it's dumb guys like you who make it easier."

Then this guy punched me, just once, a hard fast blow which landed in my guts and made me double up. I fought to draw in breath while he yanked back my head by dragging on my hair.

"You're a white man. Don't let your people down. They'll only be your friends till you betray your own. It's lucky that we heard, since you don't really want to let us down, do you?"

I didn't answer so he jerked my torn scalp back, "We're your friends," he said. "Who are your friends?" he asked.

I whispered, "You're my friends . . ."

"That's right. And we'll be sticking around to keep an eye on you."

I'm such a hero, that's why tears filled my eyes. That's why I crouched and gasped as they walked away. That's why all I could do, when they had disappeared, was shout "Get lost!" at them.

I couldn't stand up and shout "*You dirty creeps!*" because I lack the nerve to take such morons on. I'd rather slink away, bearing my own deep shame that I'd let Carlton down.

What could I do, though? Those guys could murder me. Those guys could pick me up and toss me like a doll. Am I supposed to die to defend what's right?

I could die anyway.

# 29

Ten minutes after that I was up in my room, shaking. I had the kind of shudders you see in kids' cartoons – the kind of shaking hands which can't hold a drink. I had a pain inside like that guy's plunging fist had bust my stomach walls.

I sipped some water, which did no good at all. I had to phone Tish. My mother was on the couch, watching a late night film, and suspected nothing.

"Two guys attacked me—"

"What?"

"On my way back home. I was working at Joe's—"

"Are you okay?" she asked.

"Yes, I'm not really hurt, but I'm a bit upset. One of them hammered me."

"Where did he hurt you?"

"He punched me in the guts. My stomach really hurts—"

"He might have burst something. Have you phoned for the police?"

"The police would laugh at me. I'd have to get killed first."

Tish sounded concerned. "Do you want me to come round?"

"I'll be okay," I lied. (I still wanted to cry.)

"Do you know who the men were?"

"Just two big blokes," I gasped, as pain ran through my groin.

"Do you think you'd recognize them?"

"Oh sure, I won't forget. In fact they're hanging round to keep an eye on me. They said they're watching out to see what friends I keep. Like, I should have *white* friends."

Tish sounded puzzled. "What do you mean?" she asked.

"If you play on the team you wear the uniform."

"I don't get this," she said.

"It's pretty clear," I said. "Those guys were racists."

"But you're not like that—"

"That's the whole point," I sighed. (*Heck, is she getting this or have I lost my mind?*) "Those guys were warning me to dump off all my friends who don't peel in the sun."

"You mean like Carlton?"

"Yes. Carlton's black," I said.

"So what are you going to do?"

"What do you think?" I asked. "You can't give up your friends just 'cause some guys come round who don't approve of them."

"But they might hurt you."

"I'll keep out of their way."

"Those men should be locked up."

"Something like that," I said.

"Are you sure you're okay?"

"Oh yes, I'm fine," I lied. (Inside, I'm terrified.)

I want to curl up: I want to run and hide. I want to

take a gun and make those racists die. I want to find a world where you don't feel afraid because of the friends you've got.

Who are these people who want to screw things up, who make you feel so dumb and chewed up by your doubts? So many nasty guys just hang around to pounce. So many men tell lies.

"I thought you might have called at Joe's this afternoon," I murmured quietly.

"I had to go out. I had something to do."

"Where did you go?" I asked.

"Nowhere particular."

(*Nowhere particular.* Why did my spirits sink beneath those little words?) "Was this with Paula?"

"I went on my own," she said.

"Did you find something nice?"

"Not very much," she said.

(My mind flashed *This is it, she's found somebody new.*)

"Tomorrow night," she said.

# 30

I have two great fears which undermine my life and make relaxing hard.

I'm scared of dying in agonizing ways, and even worse than that, I'm scared of staying alive.

I don't know which is worse. I don't know which hurts most.

My girlfriend hates me. (*So why's she coming round tomorrow?*)

Two big guys beat me up. (*But you're still alive.*)

My stomach hurts like hell. (*Go choke some aspirin down.*)

God, it's hard being me . . .

# 31

I lie in hot darkness thinking of beatings up and Tish's love for me. I know she likes me but I still can't relax – jealousy rears up at every chance it gets. It gnaws away at me and makes me say strange things, as if I'm daring her. Like trying to goad her to fall for someone else, just so I can turn round and say "I told you so." I don't know why it is that falling for someone brings all this doubt with it.

It's insecurity, that's the main cause of it – looking at other guys, thinking they're better than me. I don't know why this is, because it's me that Tish is going out with. I'm scared of losing her and being on my own, afraid that no one else will ever fancy me. Yet I like other girls, and half the time I wish that I could be with them.

I want the whole world. I want Tish and the rest. I want to be a swine and go with other girls just so long as Tish doesn't know; just so I'm not caught out and have a scene face to face.

I like Carlton's sister, who's twelve months younger than me. I like the way she laughs, and how she smiles at me. I like to lie in bed and think of Alfia, and what she's doing now.

I wish she'd come to me as if by magic charm, drifting into my room to sit beside my bed. I wish she'd reach her hand to stroke across my chest, and bend her face to me.

I'd like to kiss her, and feel her kiss me back. I'd like to taste her tongue, her lips, her chest, her warmth. (I'd like to fall asleep before these dreams of her keep me awake all night.)

Why is it so complex that, writhing over Tish, I still have horny dreams about somebody else? I just want all the world, every girl ever born. And half their mothers too.

Yet while I'm dreaming, just drifting on the bed, I hear sounds down below. Someone's singing a mindless racist song, singing "Go home you blacks" to the tune of "Auld Lang Syne". Smashing their Holsten Pils bottles against the walls of the Schuster block.

I hear a car start and quickly drive away. Somebody

joyriding, or someone out too late in the wrong part of town, where you don't hang around, where night hawks stalk the streets.

I hear a car backfire. Or maybe it's a gun. I've heard guns before; I've seen lights shot out. I hear somebody scream. A scream, it's hard to tell if it's alive or not.

"Are you all right, Mum?" I murmured quietly, outside the bathroom door. "Do you want some water?"

"No, I'm, all right, Stevie. Go back to bed," she said.

"What will you do?" (She hasn't been to bed. The mix of drugs and booze makes her lose track of time.) "You've left your supper out."

"I don't want to eat anything. Just throw it in the bin."

I waited, leaning my head against the door, picturing the pink bath tiles which we put up ourselves. The new shower-curtain rail, the little dish for soap . . .

"Are you coming out?" I asked.

# 32

Early the next morning some Council guys moved in to clear out Bunny's flat. I was on the landing when the first two blokes appeared, let themselves in with keys and cleared the rabbits out. They packed them in a cage which fitted in a van sat downstairs waiting.

They were quite grim guys, as if they'd looked ahead to see the bleak future awaiting Bunny's pets. No Wimbledon Common for them; those rex were ending up inside a furnace-heart.

They'd go down screaming, not knowing why they died; but pets are only there as long as someone cares. Nobody cared enough to save them from their fate. Nobody loved enough.

As I stood watching, a batch of new men came – men dressed in thick green boots and dark brown overalls. They strode in through the door and began crashing round as they collected things.

Bunny's existence was being packed away, as if it was ensured that he'd be gone for good. No markers would be left to say that Bunny Scott had ever lived there.

It all seemed premature, since Bunny might be back, but I don't think the Council had considered that. They saw an empty space and thought – *We can have that –* and moved to claim it back.

It wasn't only me who thought this was wrong; several others appeared threatening and grumbling. Old Mrs Day-Bridges grumbled the loudest of all. She liked Bunny a lot.

She got quite angry, which took me by surprise, because she's a quiet old dame who seldom raises her voice. But this time she was moved, and turned on the guy supervising the changeover.

"What are you doing?" she asked.

"We're taking back this flat. It's Council policy."

"What about the owner?"

"The owner isn't here, and even if he was he's here illegally. This flat is meant for two, and he's been breeding rats."

"They're castor rex," she said.

"You can't keep rats here," the man said patiently.

"I've got an old budgie."

"Good luck."

"Do you want that too?"

"Budgies aren't vermin."

"Nor's castor rex," she said. "They're rabbits, and they're pets."

The man gazed skywards. "You can't keep pets in here."

"What can we keep?" she asked.

"This is a waste of time."

"Why?"

"Because it's cut and dried. Mr Scott should have moved out when his mother died. There's a Council waiting list."

Mrs Day-Bridges (it's odd but that's her name) seemed less than overwhelmed by this talk of waiting lists. "You've got a job," she said. "We've got no jobs round here. Where's he supposed to live?"

"That's not my problem."

"What is?"

"This Council flat. Checking that the law's obeyed while taking back the same. Ensuring that all goods are safely packed away for Mr Scott to claim."

"Big deal. And then what?" said Mrs Day-Bridges. "He lives out on the street?"

"He joins the housing list."

"You mean the waiting list?"

"That's how it works," he said. "There's a waiting list."

I stared around me at the crowd which had gathered, finding this interesting yet inevitable. You just can't breed rabbits and get away with it. Councils don't like that much.

So Bunny got moved on, although he wasn't even to know about it. Bunny was locked up because of an anonymous phone call which said he was the one the police were looking for. The police appeared quite glad to have someone to blame, and had wrapped up the case . . .

# 33

"Do you want to bet on that?"

"Come on, Carlton," I said. "You can't make bets

like that." We were inside an arcade, playing a shoot-out game which Carlton seemed to suss a lot quicker than me. He'd scored eight, while I had just hit three. Games aren't my forte.

But he'd confused me by offering me a bet that our last maths teacher would soon go out with him. The woman's thirty-eight and has two sons our age. Carlton's in cuckoo-land.

"She really likes me."

"I like you too, Carlton, but that's not the same as wanting to go out."

"Her husband disappeared."

"I know, you told me that. He's in the Army."

"Not the Army – the *Mormon* army. He signed up with some cult as an evangelist. He's in the States somewhere."

"Good luck to him."

"He's signing up to be a missionary."

I hit my button, and my whole ship blew up. "This game – you can't blow up by doing that," I said. "This game's too complex. What's that white button there?"

"Something disgusting."

As my ship glowed red a movement at my side became a friend of ours, Winston Brown. He doesn't say too much, but when he does give forth there's thought behind it.

He owns this bad leg, which makes him limp a bit, but you can't see much wrong if you examine it. He says it's just too short to match the other one, but he might put that on.

He said, "This geezer said the police found rabbit fur sticking to Ricky's boots."

That one confused me, and I glanced up at him. "I thought at first you said they were tipped off," I said.

"Yeah." Winston's head inclined. "They had a phone tip-off, then found the rabbit fur."

"An iffy phone call," Carlton said scornfully. "And then they found the fur – oh yeah, I'll go for that."

"They could have traced the call—"

"Oh, sure. Where are we, Win? This ain't America."

Carlton rose slowly from the fading game screen, and half-shaded his eyes as he stared round the place. "But I can see it now, it all makes sense," he said, somewhat sarcastically.

Winston Brown just shrugged. "That's what I heard," he said. "This geezer that I met down at the laundromat."

"What were you doing there?"

"Tried to hold up the place. I need to buy a car."

(We didn't ask why, but knowing Winston Brown there'd be a good reason why he would want a car. I think he might go far – he seems to have the knack of meeting smart people.)

"But they were cleaned out," he went on. "What gives here?"

"We're killing time."

Peter Beere

"Some guys are going to meet to form an action group."

"What – just to buy a car?"

"No, to get Bunny out and hire solicitors."

"Where did you hear that from?"

"MacReadie's got involved." (He's our local Youth Worker.)

Winston leaned forward. "What's that white knob there?"

"It's not a knob at all – it's someone's used condom."

"They've stuck it down a hole."

"They must have done it here, right over this machine."

So that kept us talking about how much sex we get, and I didn't want to let Tish down, but still had to compete. I threw a few bits in which weren't strictly true, but sounded pretty good. . .


# 34


When I left work the next day I saw my dad waiting for me. He'll sometimes do this – turn up out of the blue. He waits outside Joe's place till I get off from work. He never comes inside, although he's sometimes stood around for an hour or more.

Why does he do it? It isn't for me, I think sometimes. I think it's to get back with Mum. I think he misses her and hopes I'll put a good word in.

He never says this, but that's the sense I get. He's dreaming in his sleep – I'll never mention him. My mum's life's hard enough without *him* coming back each time he's lonely.

But at least he was smarter than the last time he appeared. Sometimes he's so scruffy it's like meeting a tramp. At least his sleeves weren't torn, at least his shirt was clean. He didn't smell this time.

He gave his usual smile. "How are you doing, Steve?"

"I'm doing okay, I guess."

"Is your mother all right?"

"She's still alive," I said. *No thanks to you, you creep. Why don't you leave well alone?*

"I just came by today to see how you're getting on."

"Well – I'm okay," I said.

The old guy nodded. "Are you still working here?"

*No, I'm just dropping by because I miss the place.*

"Smoking Joe still the same?"

"Yes, he's still going on." (I'm feeling taciturn.)

We both stood blinking, 'cause it was such a day. The sun was beating down over the Ridge Estate. The thick air stank of oil, hot tarmac and dog turds. Food litter lay in heaps.

Thick beads of slimy sweat rolled down my old man's

upper lip and glistened on his cheek. Dark stains beneath his arms showed that he'd need fresh deodorant pretty soon.

He's quite a thin man, and looked his thinnest yet. It looked like one stiff breeze would blast him off his feet. His face was lightly tanned, but that couldn't conceal the creases brooding there.

"Should we go for a walk?"

"Why not?"

That's all we do. We go for pointless walks . . .

# 35

"What are you planning to do?" he asked.

"When?"

"Now you've finished school. Will you go back again?"

I threw a stone in the water. We'd walked down to the park, and were watching the ducks steaming across the pond.

I threw another one. He threw one after me.

"I can't decide just yet."

"It's so important you do the best you can. I mean, to get the things you want – the things you need. It's so much harder now – I mean, if you leave school – to get your A levels."

I didn't care much.

"What do I need them for?"

"I don't know . . ." He clammed up, unsure of what to say. I mean, as rôle model, he's hardly what you'd choose. How much advice can he give?

"The universities. Go and take a degree . . ."

I watched this thin old guy go jogging round the park. Old guys as frail as that, you think they're gonna croak when they go stumbling by.

"What good will that do? There aren't any jobs around."

"No, that's ridiculous. There's always jobs to do."

"I get so bored with school."

"What do you want to do?"

"Search me," I murmured.

Then I saw this old dame putting spaghetti out, and all these birds appeared, and stray cats and dogs and things. This old Italian dame had made a little chunk of Camberwell like home.

My father took my arm and turned my face to his, and I smelled whisky breath.

"You're a bright kid—"

*And you're a total jerk.* "What are you doing here?"

His grey eyes looked confused. "What do you mean?" he asked.

"I mean, why are you here? You never come round

here. This is, what? Three times in the last eighteen months? What made you come today—"

"I sent letters," he said.

"Yeah." (One. Or was it two?)

"I sent a Christmas card."

"Yeah." (But not last Christmas.)

"I'm still your father, Steve."

I took a deep breath. "Yes, you're my dad," I sighed. "So tell me why you're here."

"I wanted to see you."

"You're missing Mum," I tried.

"That's partly why I came. You see – there's someone else."

"What do you mean?" I asked.

"I've got a new girlfriend."

"You've got a girlfriend?" (I did my parrot act.)

"Yes. She works up in town; she's a telephonist. We thought – your mum and I, we've never got divorced—"

"You flaming git!" I cried.

I think this stunned him. It took *me* by surprise, and I could feel hot tears prickling behind my eyes. God knows why this should be. I couldn't stand the guy, and Mum's well rid of him.

"You're going to dump her!"

"It was six years ago! Heck, Steve, it's awful late to bring all this up now. I mean – your mother, too, she could have found someone—"

"Yes, but she never did."

I was on my feet now, and I – I don't know what. I

felt confused and sad, and mostly pretty mad. Like, why wasn't I asked to give my views? I was just overlooked.

"You're over-reacting."

"Oh, no I'm not," I said. "I mean—" (I touched my hair, as though that somehow helped.) "It's just – you come round here to say you're getting divorced. No one consulted me!"

"I'm talking to you now!" he said. "You're the first to know."

Yes, I guess that was true, so why was I so upset? (In fact, I wasn't too upset. I couldn't give a toss.)

"So, who's this new bird?"

"She's not a bird," he said. "Her name's Caroline."

I grunted.

"We're going to get a flat."

I gave another grunt.

"You could come round," he said.

*Get lost.* "I might," I said.

"Stay for a long weekend."

I stared like he was mad. *He must be crazy. Who does he think we are?* "Yes," I said emptily, knowing full well that we would never get that far. I think he wanted me to repeat all this to get my mum upset, to make her feel jealous and see how much she'd lost. I could never explain to her, but I think what she'd lost she should have given away. "Well, that's okay then."

"I think you'd like her."

*What's he trying to do? I can't take much more of this. He's going to make me puke.* "Yes, well, I'm sure I will."

(I thought, Get real, Dad – the only time we'll meet is when Hell freezes up.)

"She's got no children—" *Well, don't you give her one.* "And she would really love it if you came over some time."

"I am quite busy though."

"Well, if you change your mind," my dad said quietly.

He wrote a number, I guess a phone number, which I tucked in my jeans and then lost later on. But I wondered what she's like, this cow he adores. I'll bet she's just a slag.

"You still don't like me."

(How could I answer him?)

"It's written on your face."


"What do you think, then?" my father said at last as we walked slowly round the park.

"Think about what?" I said.

"About my remarrying."

"It's up to you," I said.

We kept on walking, skirting the mums with prams who had brought their kids to play out in the sun, and watched them running round, treading in all the crap the dogs and pigeons left. I saw a young mum who looked a lot like Tish, and thought, *If we don't start to take precautions soon—*

"She's ten years younger than me."

"That's closer to my age."

"I guess it is," he said.

Do I dislike him? Well, I don't really know. Sometimes he's not too bad, sometimes I hate the guy. I think that probably I don't see enough of him to have much feeling.

Right now I was bored though, and my thoughts were wandering. I wished he'd just go and let me think on this. Not on his new girlfriend, but whether Tish and I should use a condom now. Somehow just doing it makes it seem natural, but if we have to talk, I don't know – it's not the same. It makes it clinical, furtive, "guilty" even. We've never talked about it.

"I know you don't like me, but it wasn't all my fault. I really tried my best. I'm still your father, Steve—"

"So you keep telling me."

"What do you think, then?"

*We ought to use something. She should go on the pill—*

"Do what you like," I said.

"You're not being much help."

"What d'you expect?" I said. "You treated us like jerks."

# 36

Carlton said, "You saw your dad?"

"Yeah. How did you know that?"

"I saw him in the street."

Carlton has a motorbike in his uncle's lock-up shed, and I was trying to help him out, getting the timing right. But it was me who did the work, while he just stood around quoting from manuals.

Carlton's quite practical, but likes to share the work, which means he stands around while I do most of it. And I'm no use at all; I can't walk down the stairs without I kill myself.

He said, "Do you like him?"

"Not too much," I replied. "He's getting married again."

"What do you think of that?"

"Nothing to me," I lied. "He can do what he likes." The cam chain snapped in half.

I leaned back sighing, sitting down on my heels, and stared despairingly at Carlton's heap of rust. "You should have saved some more and got a proper bike. One with some life in it."

And then I told him what had been troubling me, and preying on my mind ever since it occurred. I said, "The other night two big guys beat me up, simply for knowing you."

"Why, what have I done?" (I don't think he really cared.)

"It isn't what you've done, it's the fact that you're black."

"There's lots of guys like that. Black guys who talk to me don't like you either."

This kind of stunned me, because I'd never thought of that; that there were guys around who didn't like my face. Not because of who I am, but because of how I look. White-skinned and fragile.

"This 'white supremacy', it doesn't bother me. Nor do those guys of yours, who go round hating blacks. Just keep them off my back – I'm as English as them."

"It's getting worse round here . . ."

# 37

*The racist presence here on the Ridge Estate seems to be increasing. Today there was graffiti plastered on our door –* WHITE POWER BLACKS LOSE – BLACKS OUT THE WHITE BOYS WIN. *What kind of guys are these? I don't know guys like this. Or maybe, yes, I do.*

*'Cause they're around here, disguised as normal folk. Disguised as friends and kin who wouldn't harm a fly. Who hand out leaflets declaiming made-up crimes they say the blacks commit.*

*You read those leaflets, you'd think that all blacks are here to start a war to undermine our souls. To take away our homes, to turn our streets to slime, to make us into dogs.*

*One group is bollock-mad, and hangs around our school.*

*It's called* Combat 81 *and recruits slugs and jerks. They all shave off their hair, they all turn into mugs – but then they get organized.*

*It kind of scares me to know there's guys around happy to model themselves on dead Nazi freaks. What if they come to power? What if they start to pick on guys with spots, like me?*

# 38

Somebody in the café said they heard that Ricky was killed by white guys.

Now I don't know the truth of this, though he seemed pretty sure, but like all of these things you need some evidence. And no one trotted out, shouting, "*I saw it all! It wasn't Bunny Scott!*"

So what does that mean? That we're conspirators? Frightened to say something in case it all backfires?

The thing with evidence, it's no damn use unless it's backed with guts . . .

# 39

Smoking Joe dropped a fart while there was no one around, and said, "Have you seen this?"

"Have I seen what?" I asked.

"This is in the newspaper." (He turned the page around so I could take a look.) "This woman in New York who had a miscarriage, and it was half-baboon."

I looked astonished. (What *is* a miscarriage?)

"It says she got a job working at New York Zoo. She must have loved her work. It says it was her job to clean the ape house out."

"Baboons aren't apes, though."

"They're not giraffes," said Joe, as he leaned on his arms, with a bristling of hairs. "This world is really strange. You read the newspapers, you can't believe it's real." His black eyes looked up. "Do you know what I mean?" he asked.

I had to shake my head. "I've no idea," I said.

"You feel like you're outside and nothing's happening there. It's all in newspapers."

Joe switched the gas on to heat a pan of stew. (He sells it as *goulash*, though it's all stew to me.) He said, "I've been around, and all the things I've seen, still ended me up here. I've been a loner—"

"The other night—" I said.

"I've been a married man—"

"Two big guys beat me up."

"I've been – what guys?" he asked.

"Two big guys. Racist guys."

"Oh yeah, those racist guys. They pop up everywhere."

"But these guys scared me!"

"Well, yes, they would," he said. "It's best to play along. Tell them you're on their side."

"Those guys were Nazi freaks!"

"The Greeks hate Turks," he said. "We all hate somebody."

(*Is that my answer? Because the Greeks hate Turks, it makes those guys okay?*)

"Why do you hate them?"

"I don't know," Joe replied. "It's all historical, mostly before my time. It's nothing personal."

"You're really letting me down."

"This here's the world," said Joe.

# 40

Just two days after this a petrol bomb was thrown into our youth centre. It landed in the cloakroom of what had once been a church, before the health service made

it the Deaf Centre. Blood donors use the joint; toddlers'
groups go there twice a week. The old folks dance and
rave.

But every evening it opened up for us, and guys
slipped in the showers to sniff at tubes of glue. We
queued up to play pool, or crept off round the back,
fooling with shrieking girls.

On summer evenings we might all troop outside to
have a barbecue or chase balls round the park. (That
got called off last year when some girl found some freak
waving his dong at her.)

And it's a mixed place, like – there's no barriers here.
We're all just lazy kids, cruising round killing time.
We've got no blacks or whites, we're all just hanging
round. Got no "supremacy". Which made it seem
worse when the fire bomb hurtled in, 'cause who was
it meant for – was it for "us" or "them"? Which side
started a war which would blaze through our lives like
a rampant disease?

*There was a muffled smack as it smashed against a wall,
and flowed in crimson waves.*

Inside ten seconds guys' coats went up in flames.
Heat from the burning wall blew out two window panes.
Voices inside the hall half-screamed and half-acclaimed
this sudden, strange bonfire.

People went haring, with no real plan at all. They
galloped at the flames, turned and ran back again.

They shouted "Where are you?" and I thought, *Where's who*? But no one called for me.

And then some strange girl grabbed me by the arms, shouting, *"The roof's on fire!"*

"You what? The roof's on fire?"

She screamed, *"The roof's on fire?"* then darted off again, as if I'd panicked her.

I could smell petrol fumes wafting on the air, hear startled cars outside swerving round fleeing legs. I could see clouds of smoke, as if it was the start of endless forest fires.

# 41

One thing I quickly learned is, in an emergency, it's each man for himself.

Nobody helped out, no one did wondrous things. No one said, *"Save that child! Women and children first!"* No one had any thoughts but to protect themselves, and batter out of there.

We'd stomp on old men if they got in our way. We'd cut down injured dogs if they might sneak out first. We'd get a quick divorce if we were married men.

(We're pretty weak, really.)

# 42

Choking smoke and red flames rolled up the walls of our youth club, setting the roof alight.

A distant siren closed, then faded away. A policeman on the scene said, *"Everyone get back!"* Roof timbers sparked and cracked; strange cheers came from the crowd which had gathered to watch.

Carlton stood with me as someone cried out *"Gas!"* And everybody jumped, and moved a few steps back.

We were still far too close, and would have felt the full force of an explosion . . .

# 43

Poor John MacReadie, who'd had a rare night off, came down to watch the blaze. He's quite a young guy, though he looks older, because he works too hard and doesn't sleep enough. It wouldn't take too much to get him walk-on rôles as a cheap vampire.

And yet I like him, because he does his best to help us out with work and keep us out of jail.

He's got a nice girlfriend, a half-Indian girl called Angela Patel.

I saw them watching, as close up as they dared, and wandered up to them just for a friendly face.

The flame-light touched their eyes, and made Mac-Readie's face into a blood-touched mask.

"It's some mess, Steve," he said, with a complete absence of emotion in his voice.

It must have shattered him to see this place burn down; he'd spent so many hours trying to build it up. When MacReadie first arrived, no one would use the place for all the violence.

It was full of weirdos who kept spitting on his car, and smoking in the bogs, and coming out happy. Not with a happy heart, but with the happy smile of guys on cannabis.

And when the smack came things got really bad, with people hauling guards and waving blades around. Mac-Readie braved a guy who'd gone to other worlds – and got cut up for it. At that point people rallied round and forced the weirdos out, to claim it for themselves.

It must have cut him now to see that place burn down, while fools applauded.

"It was just mad," I said, trying to play it down. "Just a wild evening."

MacReadie nodded. "Yeah, it's just mad," he said. But, looking in his eyes, it went deeper than that. It wasn't simply mad, it was part of his life that got destroyed that day.

# 44

Carlton re-materialized just as my mind registered that he'd gone wandering off.

"I just saw Winston—"

"I saw him too," he said. "He said it was white lads who chucked the petrol bomb. A bunch of skins ran off just as the place went up. No one's seen them before."

"It's getting worse, you know? It's getting rough round here."

"It's just the time of year. Summer's gone on too long."

I hoped that's all it was. I hoped these times would pass when autumn leaves appeared.

# 45

My mother puked her guts while I stood helplessly, not knowing what to do.

What could I say to her? How was I supposed to act?

Was I supposed to shout and scream, *You've let me down. You're letting yourself down and all you're really doing's creating misery?*

She's set off backwards, towards that murky state where self-hatred and guilt pile years on her. So that from thirty-six she alters overnight, till she looks fifty.

Her face collapses, and it's a pretty face. I've told her in the past she has a pretty face. But she thinks she's old, and all her looks have gone, and so turns out that way.

I blame my dad now, because he cheated us. He said he would be strong and take good care of us. But he's picked up some girl who's only half his age.

I really hate my dad.

# 46

Tish wanted me to take her down to see the blackened hulk where our youth club once stood.

I said, "We've got a new place – the scout hut in the park. We can go there twice a week, if we help to patch it up."

She said, "We're getting too old to hang around youth clubs; we should do better things."

This kind of stunned me, and I said, "But why? What for? I like places like this. Where else are we going to go?"

Tish sighed and looked away, as though there were things to see much better than my face.

She pushed her hair back, and said, "There are some things we need to talk about. Let's go and find somewhere away from all this noise. Talk about the two of us."

We wandered down to the park, and every step we took made me fear what would come.

Was it all over between me and my girl? Had she found someone else who could do "better things"? Was the burned youth club a sign that our love too had died and turned to trash and ash?

As we were walking I watched a thin old man feed his loaf to the ducks, and wondered if those ducks cared for the man at all. Did they just take his bread, then float round when he left, waiting for someone new?

Do they have loyalty? I don't think so. Do they have tender hearts or no heart at all? If that man dropped down dead, would the ducks grieve for him or make off with his bread?

But all this thinking got me nowhere at all, so I just followed Tish like I'm her tag-on fool.

She said "We're sixteen now and we should start to take our lives more seriously."

I nodded glumly. (I don't like "serious".)

"We're not kids any more; we've got to plan ahead."

"Like money in the bank? You don't mean splitting up?" I asked half-heartedly.

"No, I mean *us* two—"

We sat down on a bench. *Mick and Sue* had been there first, scratching their names on it. I tried it myself once, but the whole thing takes so long I got fed up with it.

She started scraping her left toe on the ground, and I felt a bit left out 'cause I'd not thought of it. I sat there on my own, my hands shoved in my jeans, wondering what's coming next.

Finally she told me; or told me part of it. I had to guess the rest later when she'd gone home. I think she was talking about something a lot more real than I was expecting.

She said, "I think it's time we worked out what comes next. Plan what we ought to do."

I raised my left foot, and saw that the leading edge of my trainer was torn, and peeling from the sole.

"We ought to look ahead. How long have we been going out?"

"Seventeen months," I said.

I could sense her nodding, although I didn't look. "And we take lots of risks, with having sex and things. One day our luck might change, and I'll be up the spout. This is a chancy thing, and we've got to stop just fooling round with it."

I listened gravely, wondering what was to come.

She said, "We could save up and buy things for a flat. We could buy furniture, and – what do you think, Stevie? Should we two get engaged?"

# 47

I had to think on this, because my head was spinning round like it was on a wheel.

I sought the advice of the wisest man I know: my mentor, Smoking Joe – a man who's been around . . .

He took it seriously.

"This thing is pretty big. It's not like buying bread, binning it when it's stale."

"She's not a loaf, though," I said, in case he'd missed a vital point somewhere. Or I was going mad.

"You buy a loaf like this, you've got to be prepared to make sure that it lasts. Maybe you want jam—"

"I get the point," I said.

"And there ain't always jam. Or not the jam you want. Maybe it's marmalade."

"Is this a cookery lesson?"

"Did you take cookery?"

"I did a bit," I said.

He smiled triumphantly. "Well, there's my point

then! 'Cause you have to know that when you cook something you've got to live with it. You've got to *eat* the stuff—"

"She's not a cake," I said.

Joe sighed despairingly. Then he waved his hands around and let his shoulders shrug. "No, I know that," he said. "She's a fine young girl. I wish you lots of luck. I wish you happy lives. Go get those dirty plates."

# 48

*The constant threat of violence is the dark side of the coin which rolls along our streets.*

*Asians get beaten up and no one seems to care. Carlton gets dogged from school by guys brandishing knives. What kind of world is this? What kind of weirdo town will I get wed into?*

*We've got no safety wherever we go, 'cause guys wielding fear come out and track us down. Turning men against men. Impressing their own small minds with their pitiful lies.*

*It's only our own belief which keeps us on the tracks: the thought that we might win while all those guys go down.*

*That if the reckoning comes they'll all have lousy lives, while
we'll have hope at least.*

# 49

That night on my way home I saw two big skinheads
pounding an Asian guy. The guy had caught them
spraying their racist filth, and like a fool stepped in,
though they were twice his size. He'd tried to pull them
off, and they'd paid him back by altering his face.

They kicked his jaw in, and stomped down on his
face. Left him with pools of blood spreading from ear
to ear. Left him with broken hands and a half-ruptured
spleen. Left this guy blubbering.

I went to help him, though there wasn't much I could
do but crouch down in the slime of the waste ground
where he lay. A woman went for help, and a light shone
in my face. "What's that you're doing there?"

"I'm trying to help him."

"What for? He's not your kind. Whatever he
deserved, it looks like he just got."

"This bloke is really hurt."

"So what? It's not your job to play Samaritans."

I couldn't answer. I just crouched in the dark, close

by the beaten man who whimpered quietly, watching this new stranger and wondering what I'd done wrong, what it was with the guy . . .

# 50

That night while we were asleep, our letterbox was shoved back to let some pamphlets through. They were churned-out xeroxes, the colours slightly blurred. Thick printing black on white, borders deep red like blood. The bold type screaming out the *British Front* message of racial hatred.

It really chills me that these guys hate so much, and despise everyone who's not from around these parts. They hate the Jews and blacks, Asians and Africans. They hate their brothers' wives.

I can't see why, though. Why are they so upset? Why can't they give their lives to something more than that? Where did they get diseased with this cancer of the soul?

It must be a nightmare to walk round in a world where you see only hate and stacked-up enemies. The only hope they have left is to put down all their foes until nothing remains.

But I can't see this.

I just can't believe that it's the colour of men's skin. It's the colour of their souls.

# 51

That night a fair set up in Brockwell Park, and we all went to it.

Tish wore leggings and a top in yellow splashed with red. I wore my new trainers and a soft camel shirt. Carlton was dressed in black, which made him fill the night like a soft panther.

Alfia came too. She's growing up so fast I can't help fancying her. And when we met up with some mates beyond the Herne Hill gates we made up quite a crowd.

A relentless *buhm buhm buhm* roars from the speakers on the rides as we stride through the park.

My mates are with me, and so's my future bride. There's money tucked in my jeans, a night of fun ahead. My acne's fading fast, and hair's started to grow where my first stubble will be.

I feel quite handsome because I'm feeling good, and nothing can go wrong when you're as good as this. We make quite a pair, me and my girlfriend Tish. The best looking around. Also, with Alfia near I'm feeling in the state of knowing temptation's face, and that I'd like to fall. But I don't think this is wrong, as long as no one else is ever hurt by it.

I won't be like my dad, though, and leave Tish in the lurch.

We'll have our jobs and home, and our friends still around.

We'll be forever more just as we all stand now, friends to defy the world.

"Is this a fresh hotdog or some of Winston's crap?" says Carlton at my side.

We all start laughing, without a reason why. We laugh to clear our souls of the dross brought by the days. We laugh because it's hot and evening's closing in fast. And it's so bright ahead.

The waltzer whisked us round, but the guy didn't swing us, 'cause he was busy chatting up two girls.

Tish said, "Have you told her yet?"

"Who? My mum?"

She nodded.

"Not yet," I said. "I'm building up to it. Have you told your mum yet?"

"No, but I told Paula. She's sworn to secrecy."

I had my arm round her neck, and I said, "We have

kids, they'll be the best kids yet. Give them the way you look and the way I will work, they'll be unstoppable."

Tish threw her head back and her laugh was a joy. I saw her perfect teeth, white neck. I said, "I think you're the most beautiful girl I've ever seen. We could just do it – buy an engagement ring."

She said, "They ought to know."

"But they might not approve."

"Then we'll just have to prove that we know what we're doing, and we're mature enough."

I nodded. Tish is right – we have to prove this thing. Prove that we're not just kids, but people in the world. We're growing up too fast to have to apologize. We're in the adult world.

"We'll have to work, Tish."

"I know." (This seriously.)

"I'll have to find a job."

"Better than Joe's," she said.

"We'll have to buy a home, buy all the things we need."

"I've got some towels," she said.

"Is this a start then?"

"Yes, it's a start," she said. "It's called a 'bottom drawer'."

"I keep my socks in there."

"Not from now on," she said. "From now on everything we do, we do for us."

"I'm into that," I said.

Daylight lingered on inside a band of gold which split the western sky.

We splashed our money round like we were made of it. We rode on every ride like junkies of the fair. We dined on 'dogs and Coke like we'd never had a meal worth calling one.

And as the darkness closed in, the lights and music blared. Our mates went spinning round upon a Wall of Death. Me and Tish were at the top, our hands clenched like a vice which has been locked in place. I tasted candy floss lingering on her tongue, and felt a burst of lust go surging through my loins. I said, "Let's go somewhere—"

But she said, "Don't be daft; I'm not doing it round here."

Someone had brought whisky and we mixed it with our Cokes. The rush started in our heads, burning back in our throats; filled us with bravado, made us feel right and strong.

We were a wild bunch careering round the place, attracting glares and looks from the guys on patrol. But we weren't troublesome. We were just having fun. We were just being ourselves.

I saw Alfia stare at me once or twice, and thought, *I'm sure that look means that she fancies me.*

But Tish was at my side, and I was too drunk to care.

I love Tish anyway.

# 52

The close of fairground night ended up in a fight, but we weren't part of it. It was a crowd of black kids involved with white skinheads. Police cars moved in in force, like they'd been waiting for it. Just the normal affray: kids bleeding, kids upset, kids getting shoved in vans.

Things broke up quickly when the police produced their dogs, which couldn't have been fed since 1984. The way those dogs struck out . . .

Black kids outnumbered whites going into the vans. This would be okay if more were in the fight, but, at least to my eyes, skinheads outnumbered blacks. How come the police walked past and let the skins run off, then piled into the blacks?

# 53

This from a book I got from Camberwell library, about our "racist state":

*Young blacks are frequently stopped and questioned on the*

*basis of no more than a generalized suspicion that if they are black and young and on the streets they can be up to no good. And the way that blacks are subjected to violent arrest stems from another presumption: that blacks are violent and aggressive by nature and must, from the outset, be dealt with violently and aggressively.*

I mean it's rubbish, this kind of stuff, you know. You don't go beating guys just 'cause they're young and black.

The tone this author used was an ironic one.

Some guys are serious . . .

# 54

The next day John MacReadie dropped in at Joe's café to have some coffee. He dumped his briefcase on the counter and checked his attack alarm, which he keeps clipped to his belt. (It also pages him when he's not at his desk, which is most of the time.)

He was looking weary. (But then he often does.) He gnawed on chewing gum. (Giving up cigarettes.) He dropped some in the bin and said, "You at the fair?"

"Yeah. Just the usual fight. Some guys from Streatham—"

"You still going out with Tish?"

"Yes, we're getting engaged."

"Yeah? Well, that's really great."

I topped his coffee up. "Are you working today?"

"Up at the Catholic school."

He spooned in sugar, stirred it round carefully. Took more gum from his mouth, and saved it on the side. Then stared down at his hands, turned them to read his palms. His blue eyes looked quite pale.

"I saw Bunny today and he looked pretty low," he murmured to his cup.

"He must be going crazy, wondering what's going on."

"They've put him in a cell with nothing but bare walls. He shares with two other guys. It shouldn't be like that; he should be on his own." He sipped his coffee, and unwrapped some more gum. "Bunny needs proper help, he's not a criminal. He just sits and cries for hours."

"What about those other guys someone saw on the roof?"

John MacReadie's arms shrugged. "They've got no witnesses. And they're not looking too hard while they've got Bunny there."

"Do you think he'll be okay?"

"Who knows?" MacReadie sighed. "Not the way things stand right now."

# 55

My mum said, "What did you say?"

"We're getting engaged," I said. "We want to get married."

My mum hadn't been in long and was still in her blue work clothes. She was making our tea while she did some washing up. Her half-smoked cigarette burned away in the black ashtray which someone had brought back from Rome.

She filled the teapot up, and put it on the side.

"Do you want any ironing done?"

"What about what I said?"

"Do what you like," she said.

"Don't you have any views?"

"If it's what you want to do and it makes you happy, then I'm pleased," she said.

"We've picked a ring out. It's only forty quid." I sat down on the chair with the uneven leg. The chip-pan on the stove got close to boiling point, much like the day outside.

"It's a really nice one. It looks like a real sapphire."

My mother wiped her hands on the sides of her dress. She picked the teapot up, came with it to her chair. Her chair doesn't wobble, but that's 'cause where she sits the floor is on a slant.

As she picked her cigarette up she said, "I met a

man. He seems quite a nice chap, despite his big moustache. He works on North Sea rigs. He said he wrote some books on fish to pass the time."

I said, "Where'd you meet him? Inside the laundry?"

"He was washing his clothes. He used the drier twice."

(This is quite a big thing, to use the drier twice. It means "particular".)

As my mum poured the tea out she looked serene and calm. She didn't spill a drop, which means she's off the booze. But she filled my cup too much and it all dribbled down when I tried sipping it.

"So," she said, "I said to him, 'What fish?' 'Fish in the sea,' he said. I said, 'What, fish to eat?' 'No, fish to catch,' he said. He can't fish off the rigs, but when he gets to port he hires a fishing boat. Don't you think that's strange, though – a life spent all at sea?"

I stared half-numbly back, and mumbled, "I guess so."

"I'm really pleased, Stevie, if what you want to do is get married," she said.

# 5b

I went out for a walk to think things over.

It *was* a big thing, as Joe had said. I had to work

things out and plan the way ahead. I had to find a job so we could have a home worth writing home about.

So I'm just out walking, cruising the airless streets. Checking the shine on cars, the rhythm of my feet. Watching the sleek taut thighs of girls walking my way, hazy dreams in my head.

And then a voice comes, speaking out of the blue. Catching me so surprised that I jump visibly. But it's just Alfia, who's standing at a bus stop, her ice skates on her arm.

"Hello there, Steven." She gives a Bambi smile. She's got the biggest eyes you've ever seen. They're so soft and brown they tie you up in knots.

"Where are you off to?" she says.

"Nowhere particular." (It's clear where she's going. She ice skates twice a week, across at Streatham rink.)

"I'm going ice skating."

"I figured that," I said.

She said, "Do you want to come?"

I stammered, lost for words.

"I won't bite you, you know."

"I know, it's—" (Blooming heck! This girl's taunting me.)

I really like her; I like her quite a lot. In fact, I fancy her, though she's younger than Tish. And I'm getting engaged to Tish; I can't like other girls.

"I'm—"

"Scared what Tish might say?"

Alfia kept on smiling with those enormous eyes. Her tights hugged her firm thighs like they'd fallen in love. I thought, *Oh blooming heck! I really fancy her. What am I going to do?*

"It's a really hot day," I mumbled, buying time while my thoughts performed cartwheels round the curves of my head. "You waiting at this stop?"

"Yes, for a bus," she said. "'Cause it's too far to walk."

I acted brain dead. "I guess it is," I said.

"You'd really have good fun. Why don't you come?" she asked.

"Carlton won't like it much—"

Alfia tossed back her head, and laughed like rushing streams. She looked so gorgeous, so happy, so carefree.

"I really would," I cried. "It's just, I can't go now—"

"Well, come on Friday then."

(That put me on the spot. Can I tell lies to Tish?)

"Meet me on Friday."

(Can I tell lies to Tish?)

"Meet me at three o'clock."

(If I tried really hard.)

"Be here at three o'clock."

(If I tried *really* hard.)

"Okay," I stammered back.

# 57

"You're going *where*?" said Tish, giving the kind of look that Doubting Thomas wore.

"I'm going ice skating. Just to see what it's like."

"Why not take me with you?"

"I wanted to be sure. You know, if I'm no good, I don't want people there, you know, to laugh at me."

She still looked doubtful. "So what? They're closing down? You've got it to yourself so you can have a go?"

My mind ran out of words as I stared at her face, my desperation caught. I was hoping fervently that my conscience didn't show. I thought, *Don't look inside my heart and see the truth in there. Don't read inside my thoughts and find this web of lies I'm weaving round myself.*

My scared lips fumbled. "I just want to be sure."

"Okay. But I could come – I promise I won't laugh."

"I'm going with someone."

"Who?" (Her smile faded.)

"Carlton," I blurted out.

There came a silence.

"You're going with Carlton?"

"Yeah. Carlton's got this thing about trying skating."

"And so you're going too?"

"Yeah. Just to try it out. To prop him up," I said.

Tish kept on staring.

"He's scared that he might fall."

"You must think I'm stupid."

(No, but I think I am.)

"You're going ice skating to help prop Carlton up?"

"Something like that," I sighed.

# 58

(By the time Friday came round my heart chickened out. I watched TV instead.)

# 59

The news that Bunny Scott had gone and hanged himself came as bombshell.

He'd gone and done it inside a lonely cell, using a length of cloth he'd unwound from his arm. (He'd been bandaged for a cut that they said he picked up while he was fighting.)

I was in anguish. He never said goodbye, and it was too late now to think of seeing him.

I should have gone along, I should have told the lie that all his rabbits were okay.

Poor Bunny missed that. He got nothing at all except a room with cons and MacReadie's fleeting calls.

My big mate died alone, without a pet in sight.

Tell me the sense in that.

# 60

A wave of shocked anger flooded the Ridge Estate at Bunny's needless death. A large crowd gathered outside the Brixton cells that he was taken to on the day that he was nicked. Black women with headscarves and sashes round their waists waved hastily made red banners.

Some taller black guys who looked half-uniformed in matching grey sweatshirts and dingy khaki pants stood shouting from the back while young kids beat on drums in an incensed refrain.

The police were watching, but didn't do anything; stayed safely in their halls, watched from the second floor. A copper wandered out but didn't talk for long, and wandered in again.

A stupid cameraman from the local press came and took bizarre pictures of people from ground level. (Striving for an award; going for arty shots of people with a cause.)

I stood apart from this, somewhere off to one side, seeing no one I knew or even recognized. Except I did know some, but they didn't look the same caught up in such passion.

Anger bubbled out onto cars easing past. These guys were trapped in something that was spiralling. It took them over, feeding on its own rage. Spreading like flames.

I had the feeling those flames would blaze and rage till someone doused the pain.

("You didn't go, did you?"

"Go where?"

"Go with those protestors."

"No, Mum," I told her face.)

# 61

"Have you seen the posters?"

"What posters?" I replied to Carlton's question.

"They've made some posters protesting about Bunny's death. They're putting them on the walls, hanging them in the stores. I'm going to take some round – do you want to lend a hand?"

"I'm running late for work. Have you done the café? I'll hang one up in there—"

"Well, stop off at my house on your way in to work."

I took one to the café and, with Joe out for supplies, hung it up on the door.

# 62

As soon as Joe returned he glanced towards the door and said, "Take that thing down."

"It's just a poster."

"So take it down," he said.

I turned red hot inside. "I thought you'd go along," I said.

"So now you've just found out my thoughts are still my own."

Joe put his bags down, his face round as the moon, blank as a dead TV screen. He strode into the back to wash his hands.

Water was running, but there was no sound out of

Joe. No humming, no swearing, no grunting as he stretched. No *"Anyone been in?"*, which is the usual thing when he's been gone a while.

So I put my plates down and walked round to the door, and peeled old Blu-tack off and watched the poster fall. Then I crushed it into a ball and kicked it into touch. It landed under the furthest chair, where nobody could see and only spiders walked.

Then I picked the plates up again and put them on a pile, and started washing up.

# 63

I took a bus journey across to Wimbledon Common, to look for Bunny's pets.

It was a token or something: I don't know. Just thought I'd take a look, see how they were getting on. Wandered around for hours, saw dogs and kids on bikes. No rabbits came in sight.

They were all out hiding or something, I don't know. Dealing out hands of cards for chips or cigarettes. They'd got no time to spare to see who'd come along trailing his memories.

This is me walking, my heels clipping the grass, my

hands wedged in my jeans, my cap perched on my head. My tanned face nearly clear of all those spots and things I had four weeks ago.

Finding a stone bench I paused to check the scene, calling the rabbits out, murmuring "*Chuh, chuh, chuh!*" The rabbits didn't appear, but then I wasn't sure I really wanted them to.

I wanted castors, and I might just get bucks – the big grey hairy lumps which roll around like dust. I wanted sleek brown does with eyes as big as lights on someone's Christmas tree.

Some days I'm content, though it doesn't last for long.

Sometimes I get morose, and that doesn't last either.

On that day I was sad, way down inside my soul. Like a great hole in me . . .

# 64

Sunlight lanced into my eyes as I lay on my back with Tish propped at my side. Wagons were grumbling their way up Denmark Hill. A swallow skimmed the ground as if seeking lost coins. I felt Tish's soft touch, like the breath of a lark, brushing against my arm.

We were in the main park watching a baseball game that some guys had rustled up, using a cricket ball. It nearly killed some of them, the way that ball took off. It dislocated thumbs.

Beyond this lads' game there was a line of prams, where it seemed some mothers' group was going for a walk – women in jeans and tops, their laughter trilling out like distant radios.

The guys were cheering, watching to see the women's bums. Calling them to their game, knocking the ball their way. The women played along, shouting their own age jokes, tossing the hard ball back.

"I don't want kids, though. Not for a year or two," Tish said.

"Too right," I mumbled back.

She found a long blade of grass to poke into my ear. "I do want children, though."

"Me too," I murmured back.

"I want a lot of them."

"Yeah, twelve. Something like that," I said, flat on my back.

This having kids, though – it's pretty tough these days. There's only so much space, so much world left for them. We should maybe adopt kids from some parts of the world where things are pretty bad.

I heard her clothes rustle, like soft leaves at my side. Smelled her new shampoo. Having kids. Making kids. Making things right for them. Means looking after them . . .

"I've got an interview at that shop in the square," she murmured quietly.

"Which one is that then?"

"The children's dress shop."

"Oh, yeah." *Children At Ease*. (She's tried for lots of jobs.) "What time you got to go?"

"Tomorrow afternoon, at two-fifteen," she said.


# 65

Tish didn't get the job. They gave it to some girl with "retail management" experience.


# 66

Joe said, "I saw your mum. She looks quite well today."

"She does?" I said in shock.

But Joe was right, though, 'cause that night she did look strange. She looked just like a girl as she put out my tea. The lettuce salad dripped 'cause it was still too wet.

She smiled. "He was in again today."

I muttered, "Who was?"

"The North Sea rig worker."

"Oh, yeah, the fisherman."

"He's got a son your age. He takes him on a boat, out off the Essex coast. He says they catch big sharks."

"Uh-huh."

"And sometimes rays."

"Uh-huh."

"You ought to go with them."

My eyes glanced upwards. My jaws paused in their bite. I tried to read her thoughts, see what she was holding back.

She said (not to my eyes), "He said you could go out with them one Saturday."

"Go out one Saturday? Why would I do that?" I said. "You hardly know the guy."

"No. But he's asked me out."

My mother's been asked out! Good grief! I've never known my mum go for a date.

My jaw was frozen.

"Do you want to go?" she asked.

"I don't know. What's he like?"

"Michael is very nice."

She's met some guy called Mike.

My mother's got a date.

What's the world coming to?

# 61

But underneath all this, the troubles of the Ridge are like a coming storm. You can hear it grumbling like thunder underground, or the tapping of a drum some kids found recently. They picked it up on a dump, and spent all summer cleaning the rust off it.

Sometimes it's mumbling, like footsteps in the night. Sometimes it fades away like they've got it in a car. But when the car starts up, even through all that din you hear the drum beating.

I don't sleep well now – the nights are far too close, like a clammy bedsit mate who clambers over me. I can't make him budge off – he just keeps rolling on, crushing me to the bed.

It's all so exhausting that I've no strength to try this new technique I've heard for stopping shooting off.

(The staining of the sheets is something I'm scared my mum will spot one day.)

## 68

"There's been some talk around of making up patrols to check the estate at night."

"You mean like vigilantes?"

"No, man – *security*." Carlton seemed quite upset that I'd used the term. "Things aren't so bad for you; they leave you guys alone. It's us get hit," he said.

I didn't like this, it sounded too extreme. I said, "That's not the way."

"Tell me what is," he said.

I said, "Well, I don't know. I'm just standing round here fixing your motorbike."

Carlton stared at me with a look I hadn't seen before. He sighed. "You pick your side and then you stick with it."

I looked him in the eye, and felt a chill inside.

"Whose side are you on?" I asked.

## 69

"Hello, Alfia."

"Hello, Steven," she said. "You stood me up, I think."

"Oh yes, I'm sorry. I should have called," I said. "I had to work extra, just couldn't get away."

"Well, never mind," she said. "Maybe some other time."

"Yeah." (*When Tish goes away.*).

I touched her ice skates, just for something to do. (We were at that bus stop again; found myself wandering by. The clouds above my head were as thin as Joe's custard but not nearly as pale.)

Just then her bus came, but she let it roll on by, while I still held her blades in their protective sheaths.

"These things must be hard to wear."

"I could show you," she said. "Give me the chance to try."

I took a deep breath. (This girl's wiser than me. She knows the tortured thoughts churning inside my mind.)

I said, "I really would. I'd really like you to. It's just—"

"Yeah, Tish," she said.

She took some gum out and popped it in her mouth.

"Would you like a cigarette?"

"No, I don't smoke," I said.

"We've got some gin at home."

(I've never tasted gin.) "I don't know," I replied.

But then somehow – I don't know how it happened – we're walking to her home, me carrying her skates.

I'm talking about the things which cause me hope and fear. Talking about everything . . .

# 70

"Do you want some more Coke?"

"No, it's okay," I said. "I'll burst on any more."

We were in their kitchen, which is much the same as ours, but smells of different things and has more coloured jars. The kind of fancy jars which hint they might hold more than Typhoo tea bags.

I picked a blue one and twisted off the top, thinking that I might find the secrets of the world.

But when I glanced inside there were only tea bags.

"Which brand are these?" I asked.

Inside her small bedroom the quiet day rolled on, filled with music.

She'd drawn the curtains, though it was light outside, and I was on the bed, propped up on one elbow. We were drinking warm Coke, which Alfia had laced with gin her father keeps.

I was feeling easy, and tasted peace inside. It was the quietest day that I'd spent for a while. She was so unflustered, so easy to chat to. We talked of lazy things.

"What's happened to Carlton? I haven't seen too much of him around these days."

"He's got these new mates—" Alfia rolled her eyes. She was sitting on the floor, stretching her long strong legs. "Those guys who form the groups."

"The vigilante groups?"

"The *groups*!" She gave a snort.

Then she lit a cigarette and aimed smoke at the light. (I took it from her hand but didn't like the taste.)

She said, "They're not too good. I had some other ones, but I can't find them now."

"It's very easy, you know, just being here with you."

Alfia smiled at me.

She brushed against my arm as she sat on the bed, flicking through her dance cassettes.

Warm air was around her, like a soft, safe aura. The scent which she had on, I hadn't smelled before.

She said, "These guys are good—"

I watched her big brown eyes.

And then Alfia kissed me.

It was no big deal, like no real sex took place. We just kissed on the bed, and she was soft and warm. I felt her in my arms, her body, her thin shirt . . .

"You could have me," she said.

# 71

That night I had a call. "There's going to be a fight. You'd better be there."

I didn't know him. "Who's this?" I mumbled back.

"We meet at ten o'clock outside the Green Man pub."

"I don't know who you are."

"We're beating up the blacks. Make sure you come along."

# 72

I watched from my window as shadows in the night formed into hunting groups.

Should I have phoned the police to warn them? (What good would my call do? The police would only watch.)

Or should I go along and try to sort this out? (What good would my voice do?)

Instead I hung around like someone on a fence, listening for sounds of fights, or sirens in the night.

I looked for flashing lights, survivors of gunfights on lonely street corners.

# 73

I saw John MacReadie and he said, "It's getting worse, this racial violence."

He wasn't joking: the Ridge Estate at night is like a war zone now, littered with broken glass.

The police don't seem to care, or turn a blind eye, hoping it'll fade away.

# 74

The new school term started but I didn't go back. I was hoping to find a job.

Joe said I'm crazy, and I should get A levels. I said, "I need a job so I can get married."

He pooh-poohed this idea. "You get your schooling first, and then you get money."

But I don't know, though – we're talking five more years. I've got my mum at home, I've got Tish on my mind. I ought to watch my mum, make sure she doesn't slip back to alcoholic hell.

I read a new book on kicking drugs and booze, and it doesn't seem too hard if we just take our time. Go one day at a time, taking just one less drink until she eases through.

I had a thought once that she should marry Joe, but that didn't work out 'cause he's got Mrs Joe.

But now she's got this Mike. If he can help her out, this thing could be knocked flat.

"You getting paid for this? You getting paid to dream?"

"No. Sorry, Joe," I said.

Even the café now displays the new tension. People have frightened eyes, and look like they don't sleep. The doc's doing a roaring trade in drugs like Valium. You should buy shares in them.

# 75

I can't begin to describe the shock I felt inside when Joe's café burned down.

It was a fire bomb, tossed through the front window. (He's had hatred before. People call him a "wop".) It made the night a veil of hissing sparks and smoke. A crimson funeral pyre.

I feel so helpless that all our small hopes have died and all our small-time plans seem like handfuls of smoke. Can't talk of Joe's blank eyes as he stood in the street, watching life blaze away.

I touched him on the arm.

"What, son?"

"I'm sorry, Joe."

Joe didn't answer me.

I couldn't find them, the words to bale him out, to make this awful night into just one more night. The way to say that life could begin anew, and he could start again.

He wouldn't believe it, and nor did I, I think. I thought this was the end of Joe and his few dreams.

Even my mum came down. Stood by me in the street, watching the orange flames.

# 76

The fair in Brockwell Park seems a long time ago. Was that the start of it?

There is an emptiness now in all my days. No place for me to go, no pans for me to clean. I haven't heard from Joe. I don't know where he lives to go and visit him.

I just stand staring at where those days should be, at the black, charred remains of Joe's ruined café. I'm still too upset to be angry at this. Someone has gutted me.

# 77

"Are you coming bowling tonight?"

"Where at?"

"We've got a van."

"Who else is coming?" I said.

"Alfia," said Carlton. "And a few of the guys. You could bring Tish along—"

"Yeah, I'll do that," I said.

"We're going to meet at six."

"I'll be there," I replied.

(I kind of like bowling.)

My first one veers away into the left gutter.

"That ball's wonky."

I make my backswing, and the next one hurtles out, sailing straight as a die, punching a nine-two split. I want to be the best, and feel a little miffed that I've left two up. I keep on staring, as though I'd like to bowl a third to take those last two out, then walk calmly away.

"I thought you were good," Tish says.

I say, "I thought I was."

"We're going to lose," she says.

Next up is Alfia, who really works that ball. She's wearing a black wool skirt that looks glued to her hips. She throws a long backswing, but still keeps her control, and almost clears the frame.

I can't help watching as she bends down again, her face deeply intent, dark-eyed smile flashed my way. Some old song thunders out across the sound system, called "It's a Heartbreak".

Tish says, "I hate this game. I never throw it straight. You throw the ball for me."

"But it's so easy. Just roll it at the pins. Don't

try half-lobbing it, like halfway down the lane. Just let your arm ease back, flow through, a rhythmic thing—"

"You throw for me," she sighs.

"Man, this ain't funny!" (Alfia's watching me.) "Who's nicked my purple ball?" (Carlton gets serious.)

I watch the next lane down, where some guy rolls that ball like it's on a wire. It looks so easy, and he doesn't break a sweat. His girl hands him a drink as he glides back again.

While Carlton throws his balls, guttering both attempts, and howls. (He tries too hard.)

I try to calm him.

"You're throwing it too hard."

"Get lost." He glares around, like he's defying me. "This game's no fun at all."

"You're just trying too hard."

"I want to kill those balls!"

"Are you going to tell them now?"

"About what?"

"About us getting engaged."

"Okay. I guess," I smiled.

So then I told them, and Tish said, "Look at this!" and flashed her ring around. Our whole gang hummed and cooed, high-fived and raised up stares.

Alfia watched my eyes . . .

I think it's still there, this thing that we've half

got. This tempting half-affair which can't get off the ground.

I think I love her too, and want all of the world. Just like I always do.

# 78

As I was walking Tish back to her house that night we saw more trouble. A gang of white kids was smashing up a car. (Looked like a drug guy's car; black BMW.) Some people looking on, fresh out of some party. They didn't seem to care.

The guys had long bats like kids use in the street. One was right on the roof, smashing the rear windscreen. One walked calmly round, punching out every light, caving the bonnet in.

The jet black paintwork looked like a railway map. The back seats heaved with smoke from burning newspapers. The tyres gave up the ghost as some guy with a knife punctured long holes in them.

And while this went on the party people watched, like it was some sideshow.

They didn't smile or laugh, or make a single sound. Just stood there watching it.

# 79

"Alfia fancies you."

"No way."

"She does," says Tish. "I've seen her watching you with those big lazy eyes."

"Don't be so crazy—"

"Can't take her eyes off you."

(I snuggled round my fire, hoping this wouldn't show.)

"Why should she fancy me?"

"God knows."

(Well, that was nice. Let's try deflating me!)

"You fancy *her*, too."

"I don't," I tried to lie.

"Cheap bag in flashy clothes."

"They're not flashy," I said.

"Oh, so you like her clothes—"

(Good grief. You just can't win.)

"Cheap cow."

(Alfia's not cheap.)

# 80

A guy I vaguely know stopped me in Lilford Road and said, "Joe's moved away. He's gone to Ireland, 'cause he's got family there. He said to say goodbye, and he'll send you a postcard. He said don't get upset, because these things happen sometimes. He's not bitter, he said."

I nodded silently, while this guy stared at me. A little faceless guy you could see anywhere. A thin grey shiny suit, white shirt, well-polished shoes.

"Don't judge him too harshly."

I just kept staring, not knowing what to do. Then I said, "Do you think he knows how much I cared for him?"

"Yeah, kid," the small man said. "He says that you're okay. He knows." He walked away.

And I stood watching while he walked down the street, thinking there was so much I ought to say to him.

I want to talk about Joe and what he's doing now, but the guy's disappeared.

# 81

Beefburgers, half-cooked chips, fat peas and thin white bread are what I'm served today. My mother's beaming because of that guy Mike. She says, "That fishing trip, it's on next Saturday."

I said, "I'm going out."

"Who with?"

"I'm going with Tish. There's a concert in the park."

"He's got the boat booked!" (Her disappointment's obvious.) "He can't cancel it now—"

"Well, you can go," I said.

"This trip was meant for you!"

(Yeah, so I'll meet his son.)

"I'd rather go with Tish."

Then we had a moment where nothing much was said, and I speared a fat chip, and smeared grease round my plate.

"Maybe I'll go next week."

"He's back at work next week. Back on the rigs," she says.

# 82

The trouble from the park has carried over to the streets, in running skirmishes.

Black guys from Streatham are backing up the Ridge, and white kids from outside are running with the yobs. The skinheads with the knives seem the best organized, and are running the show.

To tell the truth though, I don't know most of them. They might be from round here, but I don't think they are. I think these guys just come to have a real good fight, then fade away again.

This stuff around me, I don't know why it's here. I don't know where it's from, or where it's heading for. Some guys nailed two pigs' heads to some Asian guy's door.

What's going on round here?

# 83

A guy with short dark hair gets pummelled on the ground by skinheads dressed in cams.

I think it's Carlton, but it's some other guy, who yells out, "*Get my mum! Somebody get my mum!*"

But nobody responds, and I just slink away hoping I've not been seen.

I hope I'm dreaming, and this will fade away. I hope that life and times will get back on the tracks. But I think the tracks have got so twisted now, no one knows where they are.

People are cowering behind defensive walls, hoping these mindless thugs will get wrecked by their wars.

I want to hide out too, inside some secret place where no one knows my name.

# 84

"You cut the thing off here and push it into there."

Carlton just stares at me.

"It's quite straightforward."

(He's lost interest, I think. This beat-up motorbike is now a pain to him. The dream that Carlton had of being a dispatch rider gets further off each day.)

"Just hand it over. I'll put it in for you."

Carlton doesn't object, and thrusts it in my hands.

We're doing the ignition coil, which has got all cracked up, and bent in different parts.

"It's in the manual—"

"That manual don't make sense. Can't find my HT lead."

I slide the cap back on.

"Try the ignition now."

"It still don't work," he says.

(This thing will never work.)

After some staring I throw my spanner down and wipe off on my jeans, trying to keep my calm. This bike's not going to start. I have a deep belief that it's been cursed somehow.

"What about the cam chain?"

"I looked at that," he says.

(I'm running out of steam. This thing's not worth the time.)

"Why don't you buy a bike that costs more than the price of last week's newspapers?"

We take a breather, resting on engine blocks. His uncle deals in spares; this is a car graveyard. I smooth my sweating face and say, "We going out?"

"I can't," Carlton replies. "I've got to meet someone."

This keeps on happening; he has to "meet someone". Always some murky guy who moves in murky ways.

I say, "Are we still mates?"

"Yeah, we're still mates," he sighs.
(I'm not sure any more.)

# 85

I've started shaving, but there's so little there it's hardly worth the while. In fact I don't shave – what I do is cut myself on blades which seem so sharp they could dissect flies' wings. I need an electric one. (That goes on my Christmas list of things that I won't get.)

I've also tried condoms, so that I'm adept with them. (They're really tricky things that make your fingers stink. It's an eighteenth-century word of unknown origin. Could have called them anything.)

And one day I checked on Canada, but I've got no trade so we can't emigrate. I guess we'll stay round here till Tish and I get to the top of the Council housing list.

I tried *zucchini*, because I fancied one, and thought it was from the Middle East. Quite shattered to find out they're nothing more than underfed marrows . . .

# 86

A second spring arrived with clear bright blue skies but not that stifling heat.

It could be too late to stop things happening – the people on the Ridge are set to burst apart. It seems they have to show that their frustration hurts, whichever way it takes.

My mother's lonely, because Mike's gone away. Tish is back at school, working for her exams. Carlton has disappeared, Alfia's not around. (Tied up with school, I think.)

And me, I'm lurking, looking for my next job. Hoping to clear the debt Tish's ring put me in.

Hoping to find a safe spot so when the trouble starts, I'll be well out of it . . .

# 87

A video machine goes wild before my eyes, like self-destructing stars.

This is the first time I've beaten it, but no one's

around to share in my triumph. My mates have drawn away, Carlton doesn't call round. Friends are deserting me.

I've been abandoned to play these games alone, wondering where my friends are and if we'll ever cheer again. The victory I've scored seems like a shallow thing. Counts for nothing, really.

I've a constant feeling that teams are on the pitch, just waiting for the word to let a battle start.

Yet when the battle comes, it's those on the sidelines who'll bear the brunt of it . . .

# 88

The guy's not much like Joe, and eyes me up and down.

"You got experience?"

I'm in a new place, recently opened up, and I've come on spec to peddle my own wares. I say, "I've worked a bit, over at Joe's café."

"Place got blown up," he said.

"It wasn't *my* fault."

"I never said it was."

(This guy's six foot six, built like a brick whatsit. Got

great big tattooed hands, long slash round his left wrist.
Must have tried suicide.)

"I'm a good worker."

"You're going to have to be. We get a good crowd
here."

(*Don't give me that,* I thought. *I've seen places like this.
They're lucky to survive. Brown rats for customers.*)

"We've had a recession."

"Yes, so I've heard," I said.

"So I can't pay too much."

"You just take what you can."

The guy wiped his slick hands, shiny with grease and
sweat.

"When can you start?" he asked.

# 89

My mother's at the sink. She knows something's going
on, and says, "Don't go out tonight."

"Why not? What's happening?"

She doesn't answer me. She thinks I'm too naïve. I'm
an "idealist".

She wants to take them (the dreams inside my head)
and put them into jars like they're such precious things.

She'll put them on a shelf, take them down once in a while, give them a dusting down.

But she can't do that; I'm not an ornament. I've got a right to say when things are going wrong.

(It's just that I'm so small I can't make my voice heard above the raucous din.)

# 90

On my way round to see Tish I find I'm detouring, hanging round Alfia's flat.

I'm kind of hoping Alfia will appear, because I still can't work out my tangled thoughts for her. Do I really want her, or just a change from Tish? Am I just casting straws?

Is that what I'm doing, casting straws onto the wind, hoping that where they land is what I'm looking for? Or is someone out there arranging straws for me? Planning my life for me. . .

It could be happening – things seem to be changing fast. Last night half of the flats had their windows smashed in.

Poor John MacReadie's working overtime on constant call-outs.

"You haven't been around."

(I was standing at the door of Alfia's small flat.)

"Do you want to come in?"

"I'm not too sure," I said.

"There's no one else at home."

"I'm still not sure," I said.

She wore a tight black skirt, black lycra tights, black shoes. A tangerine silk blouse.

"I'm only working."

"Working on what?" I said.

"Some needlework for Mum. Nothing too much," she said.

"Do you want to go for a walk?"

She looked round like someone was there, then shrugged.

"Okay. Why not?" she said.

# 91

We walked down to the metal bridge over the railway tracks, without saying too much.

The sun was sinking into a bank of cloud. The sky was airforce blue as far as I could see. One small spot in the south bore a soft amber hue. (Maybe from building works.)

I heard a gull cry, and thought I smelled its home, but it was just the spray from some new cheap carwash. I really like the sea and wish that it was here, washing in front of us. . .

"I've got to go away," she said.

"Where to?"

"My uncle's place. Just outside Bristol."

I stroked the railing of the bridge.

"Is Carlton going too?"

"He's staying here," she said. "We've both got different dads—"

"I know."

"That's why I'm not as dark as Carlton is."

I helped her ease herself up onto the bridge, then stood not watching her, looking out for the sea. Staring far to the east, beyond the Essex mud. Looking for ships out there.

"What are you going to do?"

"They've got a dancing school. It's pretty good," she said.

"Has something happened?"

"Yeah, someone hassled me. Some white guys fooled around in an alley one night. It wasn't really bad, but my mum thinks it's best I go away for a while."

I still didn't look at her, but stared down at the tracks. She stared beyond my back, at something that wasn't there. I know she wasn't hurt, but I still had to ask.

"You didn't get hurt?"

The silk shirt rustled as Alfia shook her head. "They were just fooling round."

"It's still not good," I said.

(That thought that I once had, about me and Alfia, I know it's over now.)

Alfia climbed down, and leaned against my arm. "I'm going to go quite soon."

"I'll miss you," I replied.

"Well, Carlton's still around." (I felt her soft face smile, though I wasn't looking.)

"Carlton's not the same—"

"I hope!"

She pecked my cheek. Next thing, we were walking home.

(By the way, I chucked that job; the guy just ripped me off. He wanted slave labour.)


# 92


"Alfia's going away."

Tish's eyes locked on mine. "Something I said, I hope."

I don't think she meant it, though I wasn't really

sure. I think she was just upset because Alfia fancied me.

I said, "She's going away for good."

"She's really good at bowls."

"Yes."

"Better than we were."

I handed her a box of chocolates.

"I found these in the street."

"Liar." She took the box. "Are you going to come inside?"

"No. I thought I'd stay out here."

"Liar." She pulled me in.

We had a long snog in the hallway, then I peered round a door, said "Hello" to her folks. Her dad feigned fast asleep, a paper on his lap. Her mother smiled at me.

They've got a nice house, with great big lived-in rooms. Thick cushions on the chairs, curtains with fancy hoops. It looks the kind of house that rich people might have, though they're not rich people.

They're not hard up, though: TVs in every room. They've got a sound system that could reach to the moon. Their carpets aren't worn thin, and reach right to the walls. They've got a dishwasher.

Within that quiet house we have our territory. The front lounge is for us, quiet, out of the way. We won't disturb her dad. I think that, underneath, he thinks I'm a jerk.

Inside the quiet front room Tish thanked me for the sweets and peeled off her white blouse.

I held her fingers. "That's not what they're for," I said.

"I know." She nuzzled me, and sparks flashed in my groin.

We sat down on the couch, my hand touching her thigh.

"This is the aftershock."

# 93

That night things really flared across the Ridge Estate as I was walking home. I almost got caught in it, and had to make a break while a long line of youths formed rings round Carlton's block. They were chanting something I couldn't make out. They were smashing all the lights.

A mob was gathering in the darkness, its anger plain to see.

I started running, skirting the tattooed hate, the closely shaven heads, the boots, the uniforms. Keeping close to the walls, stooping, half-scuttling, trying to reach my home.

I watched a police van pull up and unload dogs. Saw a troop from the south go marching through the Grave. Saw clear shields in the street, the gear, the black visors. Near-midnight combat kit.

Inside my own block, shocked figures skittering. Eyes watching from the doors, the view down on the Grave. The light from sweeping beams, the grumble of a truck, aggressive, snarling dogs.

I saw scared old men, and kids with startled looks. Saw Mrs Day-Bridges dressed in her blue housecoat. Saw frightened, gawping mouths, the sense of shocked dismay that this was happening.

And from the dark night there came a roaring chant, the sound of breaking glass, a jumble of strange shouts.

The pounding of fast feet as police hit-squads moved in, claiming the ringleaders.

"Thank God you're back!" said Mum as I burst through the door.

She was watching from the safety of her room, curtains well drawn back, lights switched off. I pulled the curtains closed. "Keep well back from the glass."

"We're too high up here," she said.

Yet still that chanting seemed to invade the room, as though the guys were right outside, breaking down our front door. We hid, her arms round me, our faces white and drawn, inside the kitchen.

We didn't say too much; we were far too intent on the screaming from outside.

# 94

"What's going on?" she asked, as I peered out of our front door.

"It looks all over; the crowds have gone," I said. "Just some police walking round, two vans, a pack of dogs."

"Don't leave your head out there."

(I brought it back with me.) "Looks like it's over."

She said, "I warned you."

(I put the kettle on.)

"Nobody bothered me."

"No, not this time," she said.

"It might be over now."

"I think it's just begun."

We sat down shivering.

# 95

The next morning showed things were not too bad; not too much damage was done. There were some broken windows, some bloodstains on the dirt, some people scouting round, looking for souvenirs. Police vans were banked up along the high street, low profile but still around.

I put my jacket on like it was a battle shield, and went outside to look. All round the Schuster block, all round the other blocks, people were staring down.

We could smell diesel, and petrol from the bombs. We could see where the dogs had pissed themselves in the fight. We could see broken glass like crystals on a pyre of flesh-stained tarmac.

I saw black armbands and war insignia – the BF's cross and shield, the locked swords underneath. I saw a bloodstained rag.

And all around me lay the remains of war: the snapped-off blades of knives, staves which had cracked like twigs, bottles and burger packs – like someone brought their lunch, dining on takeaways.

In the far distance I saw a curl of smoke where someone was burning a tyre, like they were practising – preparing for the night which lay twelve hours ahead. Rehearsing for a war.

# 96

A shadow on the ground turned into Carlton's shape.

"How's things going, Steve?" he said.

My eyes glanced upwards, staring into his own. Seeing his taut, dark face framed by the silver sky. I said, "They're scary, Carl. Did you get through okay?"

"I kept well out of it."

I didn't believe him; I thought he'd joined the fight. I said, "Has Alfia gone?"

He said, "She's going today."

I said, "You could go too—"

"What for?" His long arms shrugged. "Why run away from it?"

I stood there nodding, thinking, *He's right really; you can't run away from this.* I said, "Those guys are hard. They seem well organized."

"Tell me," Carlton replied.

We lingered awkwardly in that fairground of war, as if all that we'd lost could somehow be replaced. As if, out in the sunny, bright day, with no threats around, we could just be ourselves. . .

"I've got to go," he said.

"Yeah." (Going away to war. Meeting his battle lords.)

"Well, you take care, Carl."

"You too. Don't get involved. This isn't your fight now."

(Thinking, *He's saying goodbye.*)

I said, "When this is through—"

"I know. You were my mate."

"Still am," I said, smiling.

# 97

I wandered home again to find my mum engaged in stocking up for a siege. She'd bought up everything a small-sized *town* might need: bags bursting at the seams, boxes of eggs like we were raising hens, so many tins and jars I got stuck in the door . . .

"I hired a cab," she said.

It got hard to distract her from stashing things away.

"What's going on?" I sighed.

My mum kept toiling. "We've got to lay in food. We don't know what they'll do next; they might close all the shops."

"The shops are all in here! We can't afford this stuff."

"It's life or death," said Mum.


# 98

We crouched in our small flat, waiting for things to start, listening for battle cries.

Police lines were gathering, hoping to kill this off. Cars wandered through the Grave, steering looters away. I head the growl of dogs locked up in white police vans.

And then a megaphone boomed out across the street, and despite my mother's fears I felt obliged to look. I joined others from the block gazing down on the scene.

Things came soon after that.

# 99

The gang came from the south, marching down Maldour Street like it possessed the world.

Blind darkness seeped down and spread out through the streets. Torch beams bounced off the walls like headstrong shooting stars. The sound of marching feet was like a distant drum beating the tread of war.

I heard some shouting as guys leapt onto cars, and a great orange *whoompf* went leaping from a Ford. Guys wrapped in black face-scarfs urged the thick hoodlums on. Police spies were watching them.

After a moment I saw John MacReadie run out, trying to calm things down by using reasoning.

He just got shoved aside by guys in combat gear, so shaved they looked quite bald.

Then I saw the front guys were clutching clubs and

knives, and they were peeling off, trying to outflank the law. It looked like our estate would be the battle zone.

"What's going on?" said Mum.

"It's gone much quieter now. Like they're afraid to move."

She shuffled forward.

"I made a cheese sandwich."

(My mum's normality keeps me stocked up inside.)

Whether things break or not, sleep will be hard to find on the Ridge Estate tonight.

# 100

"Is anything happening?"

I stirred to check the view, peering down on the Grave.

"I can't see much movement, but there's some guy walking round."

Mum's brave enough to look.

"Who's that?"

"The main police guy."

The crowds had disappeared. The war had moved away. All's quiet on our home front.

"They might be back, though."

My mum stood at my side, like we were peeping Toms, peering out through our nets.

She said, "It's just a lull."

"Could be all over now."

"Let's get some sleep," she said.

So that's what we do next, crawl off into our beds; though I can't get to sleep, for I'm so wound up inside.

I think my mum is right. I think this whole affair has hardly started yet.

# 101

The dull beating of drums, which comes on the next night, is like a funeral march.

People are gathering in other people's flats. We're crowding like the Blitz, to keep the war at bay. Old Mrs Day-Bridges and her friend Mrs Ray are in our flat with us.

I'm handing mugs round, like I'm on tea duty. I'm topping up cheap cakes so no one dares to starve. I'm keeping half an ear tuned to the street outside, playing "the man".

And if the trouble starts we're going to play some

cards. But I know I'll be there, watching the guns and flares.

This living in a war, it scares the pants off you. But it's a hypnotic thing.

"Are you going to college, Steven?"

"No, Mrs Day-Bridges."

"Oh, why not?" she said.

(*Don't ask me that*, I thought.)

I took a deep breath. "I don't know. Life and times. I think I'll get a job whether I go there or not."

"My Harold taught at school. He said the finest thing's an education."

"But times are changing."

"Not by that much," she said. "You still need all your grades."

"I could go back again. If I needed something I could go for night classes."

"That's not the same," she said.

I topped her tea up as a window broke outside. Screaming in the distance. (The screeching of an owl. We've got a tawny owl which lives on the rough waste ground, hunting for rats and things.)

"I used to have an owl."

We stared at Mrs Ray.

"Stuck down our lavatory."

I kept on staring.

"After it died," she said. (The old dear's not all there; she lives in myths and dreams.)"It died in our bathroom, trying to break through the glass. Dick flushed it down the loo."

(My mother squeezed me.)

"It wouldn't go down too well. I had to use a broom."

"Good grief!" I was forced to say.

# 102

I stood at the window, peering down on the scene. The wolves were gathering.

It was just after midnight, but things were picking up. Mrs Ray was fast asleep, curled up on our sofa. I wanted to go outside but my mum had locked the door and hidden the key.

So I stood shouting, "They're crossing Maldour Street! They've reached the High Street now! They're spreading out sideways, just before Joe's café—" (Where's my old friend Joe? Safely away from this, somewhere peaceful, I hope.)

"They're throwing smoke bombs!" (Dull echoes from the street.)

"Some poor guy on a horse – looks like he's being pulled off!"

My mum and Mrs Day-Bridges came out to look at this: the policeman off his horse.

"God – flaming Jesus!" A ball of angry flame went twisting through the air as someone's car went up.

"This time it's really it! This time it's really here!"

# 103

The main force of the mob came from the south, towards the Schuster block.

It was a broad swathe of bodies in the street: black bodies mixed with white, Asians and Greeks aboard. Badges worn on the arms, swastikas, ANC – what kind of group *was* this?

Why were they doing it? What did they hope to prove? What happened to the sides? (They were on the same side now.) The only enemy was the thin line of police which stood blocking their way.

They were chucking petrol bombs and hurling lumps of brick. They were ripping up the kerbs to throw slabs on the cars. They were setting fire to shops, looting other folks' goods. The noise was deafening.

"*Where are the police cars?*" I was really screaming

out. Those guys were coming hard, nothing stood in their way.

"They're heading towards the Grave!"

And then the police poured out, in total earnest. They were marching like Zulu warriors, beating on their shields, driving the front ranks back. But petrol bombs winged in and the police started to flap as their shields filled with flame.

It was only moments since this got off the ground, but it seemed like that war had been raging for years. Pitched battles taking place, kids running, police in chase. Smashed bodies everywhere.

"They're firing ball-bearings!" I cried as police went down and horses whirled away.

"They're using crossbows – some guy's just been shot down."

"Which guy?" my mother said, pressing close to my side.

"That guy – the *ambulance!*"

"Oh God!" (My mother cried at the guy's agony.)

Mrs Day-Bridges sobbed as she looked on the scene. Mrs Ray snapped awake, bolt upright on the couch.

"They're going to storm the Grave!"

The gangs were so organized, I found it terrifying.

A thousand rioters were pressing on the Grave. A whole brigade of hate was swarming round our walls.

An overwhelmed blue line fell back and let the mob do what it liked . . .

# 104

I had to phone Tish to tell her how I was, and see how she was doing.

"Are you okay?" I asked.

She said, "Are *you* okay?"

"Yes, it's all over now."

Her crying moved me.

"The News says they'll be back."

"I think so too," I said.

"Why don't you come round here?"

"'Cause we have to stay put. We have to watch the place. We've got two old women . . ."

Tired Council workmen were clearing up the Grave, removing bricks and poles – the rioters' ammo dump. They filled up two wagons, then trundled back for more. They were there all day, I think.

"Why don't you *both* come?"

"We have to watch the flat."

(But I was scared inside; tired from not enough sleep.)

"They're trying to burn the place. The entire Ridge Estate—"

"Please don't go out," she cried.

# 105

My dad came on the phone like he could be of some use. "Are you okay, Stevie?"

I took a deep breath. "Yes, I'm okay," I said.

"Do you want to come around?"

"What about Mum?" I asked.

"You could bring her round, too."

(Oh, sure, I can just see that. My mother and his bird sharing the same front room, cracking a Bounty bar.)

"Or I could come there."

"What for?"

"To help you out."

"We don't need your help here; we'll manage on our own."

"I'm only trying to help."

"I know, but we're okay."

Silence came down the line.

I could sense him wrestling with his worries deep inside; wanting to help us out, do something that was right. He was all choked up with feelings for his son.

"We're okay, Dad," I said.

# 106

A great boom thundered out across the unlit Grave as looters torched a shop.

A battered fire engine dodged the rocks and poles, tried to get to the blaze, retreated, veered away. It slammed across the kerb, sent rioters scattering, got hit by petrol bombs.

The burning fire engine seemed to be panicking, and police jeeps hurtled through to act as bodyguards. They tried to shield the thing as it crept from the scene, smoking and flickering.

"Move up those front ranks!" I heard a policeman cry. His guys were losing ground beneath a fresh onslaught. I couldn't stay up there: I had to find my friend, seek out Carlton.

"*Come back here, Stevie!*" I heard my mother scream, as I slipped through the door, pulling on my black jacket.

"*Come back! They'll kill you, Stevie!*" But I was in the aisle, crouching and running hard.

Another car went up, sending a ball of smoke twisting through the night sky. Bright sparks around me, filling the night like rain. I was choking on the fumes, throat gasping, eyes streaming. I was pounding down the stairs, dodging the kids and junk which half blocked-off the place.

I hit the fresh air – it was like a fog – saw a small mongrel dog cowering, too scared to move. "Oh hell!" I picked it up, dithered, then put it down, leaving it in the shade.

And then I ran out to brave the Grave itself. Crazed rioters and smoke, a scene straight out of hell. Bodies just going wild, noises burst over me. *"Oh, Christ – which way was he?"*

# 107

"Have you seen Carlton?" I cried.

"Get lost!" (A friend of mine ripped his hand from my grip.)

I squinted southwards, towards the crazed High Street, where the main rioters were fighting with the police. A new mob stormed the east, charging the Schuster block like screaming savages.

Setting my face west, I saw more gangs of youths using their catapults to put the windows out.

This wasn't racial hate – they were destroying things just for the hell of it.

Maybe it meant something, but I was too scared to care as I sprinted through the Grave, leaping the barricades. The rioters had set them up using concrete waste bins, barbed wire and old railway sleepers.

Petrol fumes choked me and smoke got in my eyes. Bodies kept jostling me, shoving me like a child. I thought I was going to fall – and then a hand gripped mine. I whirled round, startled.

"Alfia! You didn't go then? You should have gone!" I cried. The police were closing in, we were going to be swept up. She was decked out all in black, making her hard to spot. Maybe she'd sprint on through.

"What happened to Carlton? Why didn't you go?" I asked.

"My mum got too upset and made me miss the coach."

A petrol bomb arced in – it almost creamed my ear and smashed down three metres away.

The flames came spreading, spilling out on the ground. We both shrieked and dashed back to the wall. Someone high up above was throwing garbage down. A cabbage slammed by me.

"Which way is Carlton?"

"He ran off with his mates."

"This isn't racial war."

"Not any more," she cried.

It was down to "them and us", and I didn't know who was "them" and who "us" any more . . .

# 108

I want to be on a lonely beach, a million miles away. I saw this beach once, while I was on holiday. We had an old uncle who lived on the Isle of Man. A long crescent of sand ran down towards the rocks and the Irish Sea beyond.

That beach was hemmed in by hills of fern and gorse, and sheep grazed on the hills, and seabirds on the shore. There were brown and white ringed plovers, dunlins and sanderlings, and a raven in the air.

I spent some time there trying to catch a fish on some old hand-line stuff someone had lent to me. Came up with sweet F-all but still had quite a day. I can still see that place.

I heard John MacReadie cry as his girlfriend, Angela, got hammered by a brick.

Somebody bust her apart from ear to ear. Made her beautiful dress into a blood-stained smock. Smashed her down on the ground and then kicked her face in just for the hell of it.

They must have wondered what they were doing there, holding each other tight, blood pouring down their hands. They must have known the guys they'd tried so hard to help were doing this to them.

But I couldn't help them because, as I turned around, somebody running past clattered right into me. Guy slowed down just enough to aim a plastic jar and squirt stuff in my face.

# 109

"This stuff's killing me!" I cried.

"Ammonia," Alfia said quietly.

She had me bending over their kitchen sink. Her mother made us tea, spooning six sugars in. Her dad was on the phone, trying to raise the police, who weren't answering.

"I'll call your mother—"

"Yes, tell her I'm okay."

"And let me speak to her," said Carl's mum, Mrs Strong. She's a big woman who used to frighten me, but I was stupid then.

She turned to look at me. "How do you feel, Stevie?"

"Not too bad. I'll survive."

Alfia touched my arm.

"Don't paw that poor boy, girl! You find a man of your own. He's got a girl, I hear."

Mrs Strong slapped her hand. Alfia pulled a face. Both of them blew a kiss.

Then Mrs Strong checked me.

"Not blind. That's some relief. What were you doing out?"

"The same as Alfia."

"That girl's a fool," she said. "She could have got herself killed. You too. The pair of you!"

She dried me with a fluffy towel, wiped the sweat from my hair, tried to smooth out my frown. She said, "My son Carlton – he's still your friend, you know. He loves you really."

My pained face nodded. "I'm still *his* friend," I said.

"This thing's not black or white, it's people go crazy. You pen them up too long they've got to turn and fight. It's not some racist thing."

She poured out more tea, and splashed some whisky in, then said, "You drink that down to put hairs on your chest. You will stay here tonight. You can't go back out there."

"I'll find Carlton," I said.

But his mum hushed me. "No!" she said forcefully. "No one goes back outside till I say that it's safe. You are inside my home, which means you are my son. Go sit back there," she said.

# 110

It was almost five when Carlton came back home. His mother screamed at him.

"What you been doin', boy? Where you been out tonight?"

Before he said a word, she yelled, "Don't you lie to me! I've got your best friend here, went out there *looking* for you! I hope you're proud, Carlton."

"It wasn't my fault—"

"*What?* Don't you mess me now!"

She clipped him round the ear.

(I haven't seen that for a while.)

"You and your new smart friends! Would they come looking for you? Would they, huh? Don't you lie!"

Carlton kept grinning as he dodged a rain of blows. Said, "Did you see much blood?"

"Too much for me," I sighed.

His mother gave a *humph*! "*Too much?*"

His dad stood by, quietly protecting us.

# 1/1

But then it came again, another night of war.

We were all going crazy locked up inside our flats. We felt we were under siege and no one cared for us. We were on our own TVs, but the way they talked about us didn't relate to us.

They were only watching us, like we were the latest trend, the flavour of the month who'd pass when they got bored. No one came down to ask how we all felt ourselves. It was hypocrisy.

They talked of racists and fascists on the streets. They talked of lack of jobs and opportunities.

That's only part of it. I'll tell you what it was. People went crazy.

It was as simple as falling off a log. People just lost their minds and thought they'd wreck the place. There was no excuse for that: it was not some sane affair. You only had to check their eyes.

They were all mad eyes – mad-angry or mad-scared. They were either eyes of hate, or eyes hiding away. The eyes lead to the soul, and in those eyes I saw a total emptiness.

This lousy world left us with nothing but our hearts, and when those hearts caved in we got no other support. People abandoned us in fear – let us fight, let us die. They didn't care for us.

But then, why should they? We're just the Ridge Estate. We don't climb up the charts or bang in winning goals. We just feed off the state, taking all we can steal.

(No wonder we're half mad.)

# /12

*Boom! Boom!* Thudding explosions come, ringing out through the night, but now we're used to them.

I'm back out here, feeling I have to watch. I have to watch this death of something I have known. I have to see my friends, their homes, their way of life, blasted away in flames.

Police lines are gathering, like it's the same old thing. Bringing up new reserves with their clean riot shields. John MacReadie's on the streets, trying to clear things up, but he might as well go home.

This will all blow away in much the way it came, and we'll go back to school, to work or to benefits.

I'll get married to Tish and we'll raise kids of our own.

Go stick this riot state . . .